THE YOUNG
CRICKETER'S TUTOR

THE YOUNG

CRICKETER'S TUTOR;

COMPRISING

FULL DIRECTIONS FOR PLAYING THE ELEGANT AND
MANLY GAME OF

CRICKET;

WITH A COMPLETE VERSION OF ITS LAWS
AND REGULATIONS :

By JOHN NYREN

*A Player in the celebrated Old Hambledon Club, and in the
Mary-le-Bone Club.*

TO WHICH IS ADDED

"THE CRICKETERS OF MY TIME,"

OR,

RECOLLECTIONS OF THE MOST FAMOUS OLD
PLAYERS

BY THE SAME AUTHOR

with an Introduction by John Arlott

THE WHOLE COLLECTED AND EDITED

By CHARLES COWDEN CLARKE.

PUBLISHED BY

DAVIS-POYNTER LIMITED, LONDON

1974

ISBN 0 7067 0144 5

Text layout by Michael Jarvis

Printed in Great Britain by
Bristol Typesetting Company Limited
Barton Manor, Bristol

single word is enough for the unassailable classics – 'Pickwick', 'Hoyle', 'Bovary', 'Aubrey', 'Jude', 'Selborne', 'Whitaker', 'Gulliver', 'Romeo'. So, although the title-page of *The Young Cricketer's Tutor* by John Nyren runs to twenty-three lines, it is known simply as 'Nyren'.

This is the enduring work of cricket literature. Before it was published – in 1833 – the few cricket books had been of scores or elementary instruction. After it, nothing of comparable imaginative or literary standing was written on the game until Sir Neville Cardus's early reports, in the nineteen-twenties. It is arguable that there is no more evocative writing in English about any sport. Yet Nyren has from time to time been allowed to fall out of print: and has not now been generally available since the limited edition of 1948.

Crucially, it has the validity of true literature in the accuracy of observation, sensitivity of feeling and sympathy of expression which makes the Hambledon village cricketers of the eighteenth century credible and relishable human beings in the twentieth – even for a reader with no knowledge of cricket.

It is surprising to find such qualities in a book which is padded – yet still physically slight – hybrid, and 'ghosted'. The first edition, even with its verbatim printing of the laws, rambling index and list of MCC members, ran only to 126 pages of small octavo. It falls into two separate halves; the first, though unusual for its early date, is no more than simple – if often illuminating – technical advice to boys aspiring to play this game. The second, upon which its reputation rests, is the series of sketches entitled 'The Cricketers of My Time' which had already appeared as feature articles in *The Examiner* during 1832. According to the Introduction they were 'collected at the desire of a few friends and published here'. It is impossible now to know how the *Tutor* was originally envisaged; whether as an instruction manual – on the lines of Boxall's earlier and successful booklet – bulked out by reprinting the reminiscences; or as the 12,000 words of recollection filled out by as much again of 'how to play'.

The title page modifies 'by John Nyren' with 'The Whole collected and edited by Charles Cowden Clarke'. Nyren had an almost unique knowledge of Hambledon cricket. His father, Richard, was captain of the club during its formative and finest period, and John himself grew up among its players to become one of them.

The son was a keen and knowledgeable, but not a great, cricketer. He was only fourteen in 1778 when he joined the hired players of Hambledon as 'a sort of farmer's pony'. He remained there until 1791, the end of the club's great days, when the family went to London. He was a left-handed batsman and considered a brave and good field at point or midwicket. On his first recorded appearance he was the highest scorer in a match between 'Five of Hambledon and Five of West Kent (with Minshull)' in which the other nine players were all outstanding performers. He certainly played in two eleven-a-side matches for Hambledon and possibly in two others – where the ommission of initials renders it unclear whether 'Nyren' is John or his father – without making any appreciable score. After he went to London he played in some thirty matches – generally for Homerton, though once for England against Surrey – important enough for the scores to have survived, and, by the standards of the time, often batted valuably.

Clarke, in the second edition of the *Tutor*, described him

as 'a remarkably well-grown man, standing nearly six feet, of large proportions throughout, big-boned, strong and active. He had a bald, bullet head, a prominent forehead, small features and little sunken eyes. His smile was as sincere as an infant's. If there were any deception in him, Nature herself was to blame in giving him those insignificant shrouded eyes. They made no *show* of observation, but they were perfect ministers to their master. Not a thing, not a motion escaped them in a company, however numerous. My old friend was a "good Catholic": I mean "good" in the true sense of the word, for a more single- and gentle-hearted yet thoroughly manly man I never knew. He possessed an instinctive admiration of everything good and tasteful both in nature and art. He scarcely ever spoke of himself and this modesty will be observed throughout his little Book. He had not a spark of envy; and, like all men of real talent, he always spoke in terms of honest admiration of the merits of others.'

Leigh Hunt in his review of the *Tutor* wrote 'He is still a sort of youth at seventy, hale and vigorous and with a merry twinkle of his eye, in spite of an accident some years ago – a fall – that would have shattered most men of his age to pieces.'

Nyren made friends easily; he found it less easy to make money. He was a calico printer, at one time in a substantial way of business, but he never recovered financially after his factory was burnt down. He died on 28 June, 1837 in the old royal palace at Bromley, in Middlesex, where he had been living with his son and where he walked in the garden on the last morning of his life.

Charles Cowden Clarke (1787–1877) was a well-known literary lecturer, critic and essayist, notably a student and – in the best sense – popularizer of Shakespeare. The son of a schoolmaster, at fifteen years old he taught the much younger John Keats, then a pupil at his father's school and who later wrote his appreciative 'Epistle to Charles Cowden Clarke.' After his father's death he set up in London as a bookseller and publisher and became friendly with Leigh Hunt – through whom he met Charles and Mary Lamb, Shelley, Hazlitt – and the musician Vincent Novello. He made a notably happy marriage with Novello's daughter, Mary – who compiled the well-known *Concordance* to Shakespeare's plays – went into partnership in publishing with his son, and met the musically-inclined Richard Nyren. Clarke became an outstandingly successful lecturer and public reader; and a faithful and perceptive editor – of most of the major English poets – before he retired first to Nice and then to Genoa, where he died in 1877.

Nyren was sixty-seven when he recalled the cricket and cricketers of his youth and early manhood within Clarke's hearing. Whether the quality of the *Tutor* stems from the original speech or the subsequent editing cannot be known. Certainly both wrote independently – Clarke widely, Nyren in Leigh Hunt's *London Journal* – without approaching the excellence of 'The Cricketers of My Time'. In the preface to the second edition of the *Tutor*, published after Nyren's death, Clarke called him 'the amiable Father' of it and said it was 'compiled from unconnected scraps and reminiscences during conversation concerning his old playmates.' The result, though, has a greater unity than any 'scraps', and, as must be important, if not conclusive, Clarke was unable to invest the instructional part of the book with the vivid evocation of the player-sketches.

It is easy enough to detect Clarke's 'scholarly' approach in the quotations from the Saxon and from Strutt, in the first couple of paragraphs of 'The Cricketers of My Time', but that past, the collaboration achieves complete fusion of matter and style.

Clarke's feeling about Nyren's modesty and generosity are borne out in his book: and whatever share Clarke may have had in writing it, only Nyren could have contributed the subject matter. The 'innovation of throwing instead of bowling' which provoked his indignation was the so-called 'March of Intellect system' – round-arm bowling. Until 1835 the ball had to be bowled from below the elbow. In that year the law was altered to 'below the shoulder', despite the opposition of the older generation many of whom never became reconciled to it. This change, perhaps the most technically important in the history of the game, resulted from the efforts first of John Willes and, finally, the performances of the two Sussex round-arm bowlers, William Lillywhite and James Broadbridge, in the 'Experimental Matches' of 1827.

When the *Tutor* first appeared, the Hambledon cricketers and their opponents were mostly dead and all but forgotten. Nyren's sketches gave them and their club a degree of immortality unusual in any sport. The impact of his descriptions led some subsequent writers to call Hambledon 'the birthplace of cricket' or 'the cradle of cricket' when, in fact, it was neither. The game was earlier and more strongly established in Kent, Sussex, Surrey and London than in Hampshire. Such towns and villages as Addington, Mitcham, Slindon, Henfield, Dartford and Chertsey had flourishing teams before the Hambledon club was founded – at some time between 1750 and 1760. It did not at once become established – its major successes were achieved between 1763 and 1787 – and by 1793 fashion had carried the Grand Matches away from the bare hills of the Meon Valley to London; and the club simply expired.

At Hambledon cricket first reached maturity, through straight bat strokes, length bowling and highly organized fielding. These were not new ideas; but 'Old' John Small, the Petersfield cobbler – who 'found out cricket' – was the first orthodox batsman. His shop sign read –

> *Here lives John Small*
> *Makes bat and ball*
> *Pitch a wicket, play at cricket*
> *With any man in England.*

– and he fashioned a straight-sided and shouldered bat to play straight down the line of the ball. David Harris was coached by Richard Nyren to bowl with such accuracy that he is said once to have delivered 170 balls to Tom Walker for one run. The sides of Windmill Down, the club's second ground, sloped so steeply away from the wicket that only outstanding and immaculately placed fieldsmen could prevent attacking strokes from piercing the field and racing away to the bottom of the slope (there were no boundaries then: all strokes had to be run out).

Hambledon cricket is a phenomenon within the history

of the game. Until its time cricket had been growing from a children's play to one for the poor – first of the country and then of the cities – to a diversion which wealthy patrons – some of whom played, while others merely wagered on the result – staged on their private estates. Now a group of gentlemen formed a club in the unlikely setting of Broad Halfpenny Down, a bleak hill some two miles out of Hambledon, the Bat and Ball Inn the only building near it.

It is generally accepted that the Rev. Charles Powlett – son of the third Duke of Bolton by Lavinia Fenton ('Polly Peacham') – Vicar of Itchen Abbas, founded the club. Prominent members and backers were the Earl of Winchilsea, Philip Dehany, Jervoise Clark Jervoise, the Hon. Charles Lennox (later fourth Duke of Richmond) and Henry Bonham.

The gentlemen members paid a subscription of three guineas a year. They were accommodated for lunch and sometimes dinner – on meetings and match days – by Richard Nyren – secretary of the club, and captain and master tactician of the team, and father figure to the players, landlord first of the Bat and Ball Inn and then the George down in the village.

The most remarkable historic coincidence of Hambledon cricket was the simultaneous emergence of so many outstanding cricketers among the countrymen – small farmers, cobblers, carpenters, builders, gamekeepers and potters – of so small an area. Some of them, like Beldham, Francis and the Wells brothers, came from Farnham, and the Walkers from Churt, all on the Hampshire edge of Surrey; while Noah Mann and Barber were Sussex men. The majority, however, came from Hampshire; most lived and were buried in Hambledon, Catherington or Petersfield; or in the even smaller Alresford-Ropley-Bishop's Sutton area.

Nyren ends his memories by naming the best Hambledon team of the great period with the comment, 'No eleven in England could have stood against these men; and I think they might have beaten any two-and-twenty'. In 1772, they did, in fact, beat twenty-two of England at Moulsey Hurst.

Their cricket was clearly recognizable as the game played today, though with some marked differences. Bowling was all underarm – nevertheless it could be extremely fast – and batting tended to be statuesque. The third stump was introduced – only gradually, for sporting fashion changed slowly in those times – from 1775, after 'Lumpy' three times bowled through the gap in John Small's two-stump wicket at a crucial stage of a match between 'Five of the Hambledon Club and Five of All England'. The players wore leather shoes, stockings and silk breeches. 'You would see a bump heave under the stocking and even the blood come through: I saw John Wells tear a finger-nail off against his shoe buckle in picking up a ball' said Beldham. They played in sky blue coats with black velvet collars – the letters CC (Cricketing Club) engraved on their buttons – and, in the early days, velvet caps but, when they were engaged by Lord Winchilsea, silver-laced hats.

It is clear that this team appeared under various names. They are sometimes called Hambledon and at others – usually when Beldham, Mann and Francis were not included – Hampshire; or in the colours of patrons.

A minute of 1788 runs: 'Ordered that the Players who are Paid for Practising on Windmill Down are hereby forbidden to engage themselves to play in any County or other great Matches without the Permission of the Stewards of the Hambledon Club unless such Players shall be desired to Play for the Duke of Dorset, Sir Horace Mann or any member of the Hambledon Club. Ordered that Nyren do acquaint the Players who give in their names to play in the County Eleven with the above order.' The specific reference to 'County Eleven' confirms that the titles 'Hambledon' and 'Hampshire' were virtually interchangeable: though it does not detract from the achievement of the Hambledon club in mustering such a corps of cricketers. This minute was a clear indication that London – effectively Lord's, although MCC was only in its second year – was already exerting attraction to the leading players.

In 1923 the club's manuscript minute book and account book covering the period 1772 to 1796 were made available for publication. They show the simple, near-feudal economics of the club. The waiter – named in six variations of Hunstead – was given a black hat and paid five shillings a day.

Members' dinners cost two shillings – ten with wine – port was two shillings a bottle, sherry three; the Windmill Down ground was rented from farmer Garret for £10 a year.

Crowds were large and enthusiastic. (In 1772, when Hambledon played England at Bishopsbourn, *The Kentish Gazette* reported an attendance of 15,000 to 20,000.) Stakes were huge. Nyren says that Hambledon generally played England for 500 guineas; but they undertook some matches for as much as 1,000 guineas – vast sums for those times – with invariably high side stakes. Nyren estimated that between 1772 and 1781 the club had fifty-one matches against England and won twenty-nine of them. F.S. Ashley-Cooper, the eminent early student of cricket history, calculated that on the minimal basis of published reports, Hambledon won £22,497 and lost £10,030 – exclusive of side-betting – on those games.

Against this spendthrift background, the player's pay was abject. For a one-day practice game – which for the Farnham players meant a return ride of fifty-four miles – they were paid 'four shillings if winners and three shillings if losers'. Before an away match, the club advanced one guinea for the entire team, presumably for their accommodation. When they returned, the account books show they were paid between seven and nine shillings a man for a three- or four-day match. A few years afterwards, at the beginning of the new century, when the best of the surviving Hambledon players were engaged in London they expected – for wager matches, as almost all of them were – £5 if they won, £3 when they lost.

They also may have been tipped by successful backers: and probably sometimes backed themselves to win. Nevertheless, the ludicrous discrepancy between their match-payment and the amounts they were winning for their 'patrons' could only appear an invitation to take a separate profit: and so it proved. Nyren could write 'No thought of treachery ever seemed to have entered their heads. The modern politics of trickery and "crossing" were (so far as my own experience and judgement of their actions extended) as yet a "sealed book" to the Hambledonians; what they did, they did for the love of honour and victory;

and when one (who shall be nameless) sold the birthright of his good name for a mess of pottage, he paid dearly for his bargain. It cost him the trouble of being a knave – (no trifle); the esteem of his old friends, and, what was worst of all, the respect of him who could have been his best friend – himself.' There was not, however, only one man involved. The bookmakers – who were making as much as the backers – searched out the raw young country-men in 'The Green Man and Still' in Oxford Street, where the professionals stayed when they were in London – though their pay could barely compass its prices. In his old age, 'Silver Billy' Beldham recalled playing in a strong Surrey side which seemed to have a match against All England well in hand, when he discovered the bookmakers were laying seven to four against them. 'This time, though', he said 'they lost: they laid in the belief that some Surrey men had sold the match; but then Surrey played to win.'

This was a ludicrous situation and it came to its inevitable conclusion in 1817. Lambert – the finest all round cricketer of the period – and one of his associates began to quarrel outside the pavilion windows at Lord's, each blaming the other for 'selling' matches. Their allegations fitted so closely with the events – especially the then recent and amazing defeat of England by Nottinghamshire – that the listening MCC members called them into the committee room. There they continued, in high anger, to make such convincing accusations of corruption against one another that MCC could do no other than ban them from the first-class game for the rest of their lives. At the same time bookmakers and betting were also barred from cricket grounds.

That event lay far into the future from Hambledon's great days. Their cricket then seemed a mixture of the con-vivial, epic and idyllic. The social side was a major aspect of club activity for the members. In 1772 Winchester, Salisbury and London newspapers carried the advertise-ment – 'The Gents of Broadhalfpenny Cricket Club are desired to meet at Dick Nyren's at the George at Hamble-don on Saturday the 7th November on Special Business. N.B. Dinner on Table at 3 o'clock.'

At the front of the earliest surviving minute book there is a list of:

Standing Toasts
1 The Queen's Mother
2 The King
3 Hambledon Club
4 Cricket
5 To the Immortal Memory of Madge
6 The President

All is admirably terse and obvious except 'Madge', which gave rise to much airy and inaccurate speculation until a diligent researcher discovered, in Grose's eighteenth-century *Dictionary of the Vulgar Tongue* that it meant 'The private parts of a woman.'

The records show a faithful observance of that line of the club song which runs – 'He's best who drinks most'. A wine cistern was one of the first amenities installed on Windmill Down. The classic entry in the minute book runs – 'A wet day: only three members present: nine bottles of wine'. Although the members bought their port and sherry, the table wines were generally contributed. When William Barber was landlord of the Bat and Ball he was allowed a corkage charge of 'sixpence per bottle for drinking the club wine'.

'September the fifth 1782 – An Extra Meeting to Eat Venison & Drink Bonhams and Fitzherberts Claret.'

By a decision of 1774 'If any dispute shall arise among members, should they not be silent after being desired to wave the subject of conversation by the President, the Gentlemen so disputing shall forfeit one dozen of claret to the club.' In 1795 it was decided 'on account of the high price of provisions the gentlemen present have thought proper to allow Nyren two shillings a head for each dinner instead of one'. Still the bill for forty-nine members was £39 4s – including wines. The President provided venison for the annual dinner; when J. C. Jervoise failed to do so in 1782 he was fined a buck.

The annual dinner which wound up the season apparently resulted in some accidents in the unlit countryside in 1790 for the following year the meeting 'ordered that the last meeting of the Hambledon Club be in future of a Moonlight night.'

The most historically important entry in the Hambledon Minute book is not concerned with cricket. Late in the club's history – on 29 August, 1796 at its last meeting but one – it is recorded that there were 'Three members and twelve non-subscribers (including Mr Thos Pain "Author of the Rights of Man") present. No business noted.'

This is a matter of some significance. It is not, I believe, elsewhere suggested that Tom Paine ever returned to England after 1792. In that year, having issued the second part of *The Rights of Man* he managed to take ship from Dover only half an hour before the warrant for his arrest reached the quay. In August 1796, he had been released from prison in France; recovered from illness; completed part two of *The Age of Reason*, and written the savage letter of attack on Washington which must then have made it appear improbable that he would ever again be happily received into America. He may well have wished to explore the possibility of being accepted back into England. Henry Bonham, the secretary of the Hambledon club was a Radical; and the 'twelve non-subscribers' in contrast to the mere 'three members' – a most unusal imbalance – pose an intriguing situation which presumably will never be explained. It gives the story of the Hambledon Cricket club an end as unique as its main course; for, less than a month later, the last entry in the Minute Book – for 21 September, 1796 – reads 'No Gentlemen'.

For some five years since Hambledon so nearly won their match against Twenty-two of Middlesex at Lords, the great players and 'grand matches' had been moving to London or to fresh patrons. In its subsequent matches in the eighteenth century, Hambledon is called 'Hambledon Town': the greatest of all village clubs had reached the end of its greatness. Men in Hambledon continued to play cricket; there is still a Hambledon team now but simply another village team, distinguished from others only by its historic name.

By the middle of the nineteenth century Broadhalfpenny

had been put down to plough and Windmill Down to conifers. In 1924, however, Winchester College bought Broadhalfpenny Down and devoted it once more – and in perpetuity – to cricket. The Bat and Ball Inn still stands and opposite, on the edge of the old ground there is a stone memorial to the Hambledon Cricket Club – but its living memorial is 'Nyren'.

JOHN ARLOTT

NOTES

Nyren's memory was fallible in such matters as names and dates. At first mention he dates Cotton's poem 1776, at second 1778. The name-spellings have been corrected of Sueter, Leer, Stewart, Lamborn (elsewhere Lambert is correct), Willes (he came from Kent, not Sussex) and Minshull; the date and score of Kent v All England in the 'Memoranda' have been adjusted to conform with those (accurate) in *Scores and Biographies, Vol I*.

There are, too, a few omissions. Nyren does not describe some of the leading Hambledon players like Thomas Scott and Robert Robinson – both of whom he includes in his best eleven of the club – and Richard Aubrey Veck. Neither does he mention some of their leading opponents such as Ring, Brazier and Clifford of Kent; Bedster and Edmeads of Surrey; and the quite outstanding William Fennex (Middlesex).

These notes are included for the sake of accuracy, though they must seem pedantic in relation to so warmly felt a book.

J. A.

INTRODUCTION

OF all the English athletic games, none, perhaps, presents so fine a scope for bringing into full and constant play the qualities both of the mind and body as that of Cricket. A man who is essentially stupid will not make a fine cricketer; neither will he who is not essentially active. He must be active in all his faculties – he must be active in mind to prepare for every advantage, and active in eye and limb, to avail himself of those advantages. He must be cool-tempered, and, in the best sense of the term, MANLY; for he must be able to endure fatigue, and to make light of pain; since, like all athletic sports, Cricket is not unattended with danger, resulting from inattention or inexperience; the accidents most commonly attendant upon the players at cricket arising from unwatchfulness, or slowness of eye. A short-sighted person is as unfit to become a cricketer, as one deaf would be to discriminate the most delicate gradations and varieties in tones; added to which, he must be in constant jeopardy of serious injury.

It is hoped that the present little work will be found a useful as well as entertaining companion to the young practitioner in this graceful and very exciting game. The name of NYREN was for many years held in high estimation in the cricketing world; he was the father and general of the famous old Hambledon Club, which used to hold its meetings on Broad-Halfpenny, and afterwards on Windmill Down, near to Hambledon, in Hampshire. While old Nyren directed their movements, the Club remained unrivalled, and frequently challenged all England. The most polished players that this country ever produced were members of the Hambledon Club – if John Nyren, the son of the good old patriarch, and father of this little manual, be worthy of credit; and many eminent members of the Mary-le-bone Club, both 'gentle and simple,' can attest his solid judgement, as well as his regard to truth and plain dealing. Of the former class in society, the names of LORD FREDERICK BEAUCLERCK, with Mr WARD and Mr LADBROKE, will alone form ample testimony to his fitness to speak upon such points; while his first-rate instruction, long practice, and superior accomplishment will qualify him to impart his half a century's experience to the young practitioner.

The papers entitled *The Cricketers of My Time*, which conclude the work, have already appeared in a weekly periodical. They have been collected at the desire of a few friends, and published here. If they afford any amusement to the young reader, it is to be wished that he may at the same time be led to emulate the skill of the most eminent men recorded in the different papers, and not wholly to disregard the sterling qualities of integrity, plain dealing, and good old English independence – the independence of native worth and moral rectitude, not of insolence and effrontery, which signalized many of their characters, and endeared them to their equals, while it commanded the respect of their superiors in rank and fortune.

All the players there recorded were either members or companions of the Hambledon Club, or their opponents.

As it formed no part of Mr Nyren's plan to include those of any other society, the reader will perceive why several players of recent date, equal, perhaps, in skill to those eminent veterans, have not been included. These may, possibly, be installed with their ancestors in some future edition of our little chronicle, if fate, and the Cricketers, decree in favour of a reprint.

C. C. C.

DEDICATION

TO WILLIAM WARD, ESQ

&c. &c. &c.

Dear Sir,

You have kindly consented to my wish of dedicating my little book to you, and I am much pleased that you have done so: first, because you are a countryman of my own – having lived in Hampshire; and secondly, and chiefly, because, as a Cricketer, I consider you the most worthy man of the present day to reflect credit upon my choice as a patron.

It would ill become me, Sir, in this place to allude to other weighty reasons for congratulating myself upon this point – an insignificant book of instruction – as to the best mode of excelling in an elegant relaxation, not being the most fitting medium for digressing upon unquestionedly high public worth and integrity, or private condescension and amenity: at the same time, I cannot but feel how happily such a combination of qualities in a patron must redound to my own advantage.

I have not seen much of your playing – certainly not so much as I could have wished; but so far as my observation and judgement extend, I may confidently pronounce you to be one of the *safest* players I remember to have seen. The circumstance of your rising so much above the ordinary standard in stature (your height, if I recollect, being six feet one inch), your extraordinary length of limb, your power and activity; to all which, I may add, your perfect judgement of all points in the game; have given you the superior advantages in play, and entitle you to the character I have given. As a proof of its correctness, the simple fact will suffice of your having gained the *longest hands* of any player upon record. This circumstance occurred upon the 24th and 25th of July 1820, at Mary-le-bone, when the great number of 278 runs appeared against your name, 108 more than any player ever gained: and this, be it remembered, happened after the increase of the stumps in 1817.

May you long live, Sir, to foster and take your part in our favourite amusement; and may you never relax your endeavours to restore the game to the good old principles from which, I regret to say, it has in some instances departed since the time I used to be an active member of the fraternity. You are aware that I principally allude to the practice that the modern bowlers have introduced of *throwing* the ball, although in direct infringement of a law prohibiting that action.

I beg to subscribe myself,
Dear Sir,
Your faithful Countryman,
And obedient humble Servant,

JOHN NYREN.

BROMLEY, MIDDLESEX,
March 1833.

THE YOUNG CRICKETER'S TUTOR

THE BEGINNING OF THE GAME OF CRICKET

IN commencing the game the following preliminary steps will be found requisite; first the

NUMBER OF THE PLAYERS,

which in a complete game should comprise twenty-two men, eleven on each side. The future description of their different stations in the field, and of the importance of each in his station, will convince the young practitioner that the whole arrangement has been the result both of judgement and experience. He would find it difficult to spare one of them. Upon occasions of mere practice, however, a fewer number will answer the purpose: yet I would recommend his availing himself of as many opportunities as possible of playing with the full complement in the field, and for this purpose he must necessarily enrol himself as a member of some club, which, from the late increased popularity of this very elegant and manly recreation, he will have no difficulty to accomplish. The next step to consider will be the

CHOICE OF THE GROUND

I need say no more on this head, than that the more spacious and smooth, and the shorter the turf, the better will it be adapted to the purpose. It should be kept well rolled, and if possible fed down by sheep. The nearer the centre, if the ground be good, the better will be the spot for pitching the wickets. These preliminaries being arranged, the

UMPIRES

for the two parties must be chosen, to whom all questions in dispute must be referred, and whose decree must be final. These should be men of known competence to judge all points of the game, also of good repute for honesty of mind – free from prejudice and partiality.

The umpires take their post, one at each wicket: he where the striker is should be partially behind it, so as not to interfere with the fieldsmen; and the umpire at the bowler's wicket should place himself *directly in a line* behind it, in order that he may perceive whether the ball be stopped by the striker's leg; for if such accident should happen, and the ball have been delivered *straight* to the wicket, and the batter not have touched it with his bat, any of the adverse party may require the umpire to pronounce whether he should be out or not. If the ball have not been delivered straight to the wicket, and strike the batter, he is not out. The '*Laws of Cricket*' will describe the other duties of the umpire.

PITCHING THE WICKETS

will be the next point of consideration. When two matches are played to decide the question of superiority, the party leaving home are allowed the privilege of pitching the first wickets, also the choice of going in first or not. The wickets must be pitched within thirty yards of a centre that has been previously selected by the opposing party: but if one match only, or even two matches, be contested upon the same ground, then it devolves upon the umpires to pitch the wickets. It is the duty of these to choose, to the best of their ability, such ground as will be convenient to, and for the advantage of, the two parties.

The reader is again referred for farther provision respecting the position of the wicket to the *'Laws of Cricket.'*

THE ARRANGEMENT OF THE FIELDSMEN

is the last point to be attended to previously to commencing the game. Full particulars under this head the reader will find detailed, both in the frontispiece and in the body of instructions.

THE LAWS OF CRICKET,
According with the Revision of them by the Mary-le-Bone Club in 1830.

THE BALL

must not exceed in weight five ounces and three quarters, or be less than five ounces and a half. Either party may demand a new ball at the commencement of each innings.

THE BAT

must not be more than four inches and a quarter in width at the broadest part. There are no restrictions as to the height of the bat; it may be made as tall, short, or narrow as the player chooses; twenty-one or twenty-two inches, however, will be found the most convenient height for it, independently of the handle.

THE STUMPS

must stand twenty-seven inches *above the ground*; the stems must also be of sufficient substance to prevent the ball passing between them. The bails, when united, must not exceed eight inches in length.

THE BOWLING-CREASE

must be a yard in length on each side of the stumps, and be drawn in a line with them: at each extremity of the bowling-crease there must also be a return-crease, towards the bowler at right angles.

THE POPPING-CREASE

must be four feet distant from the wicket, and extend parallel with it.

THE WICKET-KEEPER

must remain quietly at a reasonable space behind the wicket, and not stir till the bowler has delivered the ball. If any portion of his body, limbs, or head be beyond, or even over the wicket, the batter shall not be considered out, although the ball hit the wicket. The wicket-keeper also is not allowed to annoy the striker, either by noise, uncalled-for remarks, or unnecessary action.

THE WICKETS

must be pitched opposite to each other, and at the distance between them of twenty-two yards.

It is not lawful for either party during a match, without the consent of the other, to alter the ground by rolling, watering, covering, mowing, or beating. This rule is not meant to prevent the striker from beating the ground with his bat, never where he stands, during the innings, or to prevent the bowler from filling the holes, watering the ground, or using sawdust, &c., when the ground is wet.

After rain the wickets may be changed with the consent of both parties.

THE BOWLER

shall deliver the ball with one foot behind the bowling-crease, and within the return-crease, and shall bowl four balls before he changes wickets, which he shall be permitted to do but once in the same innings.

He may order the striker at his wicket to stand on which side he pleases.

If the bowler toss the ball above the striker's head, or bowl it so wide that it shall be out of distance to be played at, the umpire (even although he attempted to hit it) shall adjudge one run to the parties receiving the innings, either with or without an appeal from them; which shall be put down to the score of wide balls, and such ball shall not be reckoned as any of the four balls.

If 'No Ball!' be called by the umpire, the hitter may strike at it, and get all the runs he can, and shall not be out except by running out. In the event of no run being obtained by any other means, then one run shall be scored.

When a fresh bowler takes the ball, before he can proceed, he is not allowed more than two balls for practice; but is obliged to continue the next four in the game, before he can change for another better approved of; but when six balls are agreed to be bowled, then he must continue the six instead of four.

The ball shall be *bowled*. If it be thrown or jerked, or if any part of the hand or arm be above the elbow at the time of delivering, the umpire shall call 'No ball.'

THE STRIKER IS OUT

if the bail be bowled off, or the stumps be bowled out of the ground; or

If the ball from a stroke over or under his bat or upon his hand (but not wrists) be held before it touch the ground, although it be hugged to the body of the catcher; or

If in striking, or at any other time, while the ball shall be in play, both his feet be over the popping-crease and his wicket put down, except his bat be grounded within it; or

If in striking at the ball he hit down his wicket; or

If under pretence of running, or otherwise, either of the strikers prevent a ball from being caught, the striker of the ball is out; or

If the ball be struck, and he wilfully strike it again; or

If in running, the wicket be struck down by a throw, or by the hand or arm (with the ball in hand), before his foot, hand, or bat be grounded over the popping-crease. But if the bail be off, the stump must be struck out of the ground; or

If any part of the striker's dress knock down the wicket; or

If the striker touch or take up the ball while in play, unless at the request of the opposite party; or

If with any part of his person he stop the ball which, in the opinion of the umpire at the bowler's wicket, shall have been delivered in a straight line to the striker's wicket, and would have hit it.

If 'Lost Ball' be called, the striker shall be allowed six runs; but if more than six shall have been run before lost ball shall have been called, then the striker shall have all which have been run.

In single wicket, the striker shall be entitled to three notches for a lost ball; and the same number if a ball be stopped with a hat.

The bowler or striker may claim one minute between each ball, after its being dead.

If the batters have crossed each other, he that runs for the wicket that is put down, is out; and if they have not crossed, he that has left the wicket which is put down, is out.

When a ball is caught, no run shall be reckoned.

When a striker is run out, the notch they were running for is not to be reckoned.

When a ball has been in a bowler's or wicket-keeper's hand, it is considered as no longer in play, and the strikers need not keep within their ground till the umpire has called 'Play'; but if the player go off the ground with an intent to run before the ball is delivered, the bowler may put him out.

If the striker be hurt, he may retire from the wicket, and have his innings at any time in that innings. Another person may be allowed to stand out for him, but not to go in. No substitute in the field shall be allowed to bowl, keep wicket, stand at the point or middle wicket, or stop behind to a fast bowler, unless by the consent of the opposite party.

If any person stop the ball with his hat, the ball shall be considered dead, and the opposite party shall add five runs to their score; if any should be run, they shall have five in all.

If the ball be struck, the striker may guard his wicket either with his bat or his body.

If the striker hit the ball against his partner's wicket when he is off his ground, it is out, provided it have previously touched the bowler's or any of the fieldsmen's hands, but not otherwise.

THE UMPIRES

are the sole judges of fair and unfair play, and all disputes shall be determined by them; each at his own wicket: but in case of a catch, which the umpire at the wicket bowled from, cannot see sufficiently to decide upon, he may apply to the other umpire, whose opinion shall be conclusive.

The umpires in all matches shall pitch fair wickets, and the parties shall toss for the choice of innings.

They shall allow two minutes for each man to come in, and fifteen minutes between each innings, when the umpire shall call 'Play': the party refusing to play shall lose the match.

They are not to order a player out, unless appealed to by the adversaries.

But if the bowler's foot be not behind the bowling-crease, and within the return-crease, when he delivers the ball, they must, unasked, call 'No ball.'

If the striker run a short run, the umpire must call 'One short.'*

The umpire at the bowler's wicket is to be first applied to, to decide on all catches.

* In playing a single wicket match, if fewer than five persons are engaged at play, the batter who shall leave his ground to strike the ball shall not be allowed to score for such stroke, unless an agreement to the contrary have been previously arranged.

The umpires are not to be changed during the matches, except by the consent of both parties.

BETS

If the runs of one player be laid against those of another, the bets depend upon the *first* innings, unless otherwise specified.

If the bets be made upon both innings, and one party beat the other in one innings, the runs in the first innings shall determine the bet.

But if the other party go in a second time, then the bet must be determined by the number on the score.

INSTRUCTIONS

Having provided the young cricketer with the requisite preliminaries to prepare him for playing the game, also with a code of the laws, the next step will be to give him the result of more than fifty years' experience and actual practice among the finest players the country ever saw. Without farther preamble, therefore, I shall commence with

THE BOWLER

The three best qualities in this important person in the game are, a high delivery, an upright body, and for his balls to be pitched a proper length. Without these requisites no man can be an effective bowler.

RUNNING IN TO DELIVER THE BALL

By a little practice the proper distance to run will easily be discovered. The bowler should make a mark in the ground from which he intends to start. This mark will facilitate his treading uniformly in the same steps each time he runs to deliver his ball; he should commence at a gentle pace, and increase his speed till the ball is delivered.

The following verse of the old cricketing song, written for the Hambledon Club in the year 1776, and which will be found in another department of this little work, expresses in few words the chief excellence to be required in a bowler:

'Ye bowlers, take heed, to my precepts attend,
On you the whole fate of the game must depend.
Spare your vigour at first, now exert all your strength,
But *measure each step,* and *be sure pitch a length.*'

The best method of holding the ball to bowl, is between the thumb and fingers, firmly enough to steady it, yet that it may leave the hand with ease.

When practising, let the bowler always use, if possible, a ball of the required weight, and measure the exact distance that is settled from one wicket to the other; viz, two-and-twenty yards. If his pace be moderately fast, he should endeavour to pitch the ball about four yards and a half before the wicket: if it be slow, somewhat nearer, and in swift bowling not further off than five yards. The young practitioner cannot do better than to place a mark upon the ground at the stated distance from the wicket, according to the speed at which he intends to bowl, and to aim at that mark.

In a match, when running to bowl, he should fix his eye upon a certain spot where he is desirous the ball should pitch: there will be no difficulty in selecting an object for the purpose of a guide; either a difference in the colour of the grass, or a slight unevenness in the ground, will answer his purpose. This is a rule from which he should not deviate – all the finest bowlers I have known have pursued this plan; for, if the length be correct according to his rate of bowling, he can do no better than adhere to that distance.

He should also habituate himself to bowl with equal ease on either side of the wicket; he will experience the advantage of such practice; for he will frequently notice that the ground on one side will prove more favourable to his play than on the other: it may happen also, that upon trying the two, he will perceive the ball to rise better on one side than the other of the wicket. All these things will turn to the young bowler's account, if he play with *his head* as well as his hands. Besides, changing the side of the wicket is never agreeable to the batsman. A quick eye, with practised observation, will induce the bowler early to detect the weak points in his adversary; let him not neglect this – and then regulate his balls accordingly.

A good length ball now and then pitched a little wide of the *off*-stump, will often turn to great advantage, for it may produce a catch, when a straight one would be stopped with ease.

In his little book upon cricketing, LAMBERT has laid down some useful instruction on bowling; I cannot, however, approve of his recommending the young player to give a *twist* to his balls: for, in the first place, there are a hundred chances against his accomplishing the art, and ten hundred in favour of the practice spoiling his bowling altogether. I never perceived any twist in Lambert's own bowling, unless indeed the ground were in his favour. If the young practitioner have once gained a good high delivery, let him never run the risk of losing it; for in this department of the game it is the greatest gift he can possess.

IN PITCHING THE WICKETS

much responsibility lies upon the bowler. The chief art is, to select a situation that will suit your own style of bowling, and at the same time prove disadvantageous to your adversaries; as these two points, however, can rarely be accomplished, you can at all events pitch the wickets in such a manner as to benefit yourself. On this head I would refer the young artist to that portion of this little work, in *The Cricketers of My Time*, where the practice of the two most celebrated old bowlers, HARRIS and LUMPY, in pitching their wickets, is described, and commented on.

It is the duty of the bowler to be the wicket-keeper at his own wicket, during the intervals of his bowling. He will have many balls to stop in the field, and many a struggle will ensue between him and the batsman, one to get the run, and the other to save it.

I shall conclude this article by recapitulating the chief requisites in a bowler. In beginning to run, start gently, and increase your pace till the ball be delivered. Fix your eye on the spot where you wish the ball to pitch, keep your body upright, deliver your ball high, pitch a good length, straight to the off-stump; practise these points, succeed in them all, and you will be a first-rate bowler.

THE RIGHT-HANDED BATSMAN

Place both hands on the *middle* of the handle of the bat, near to each other, yet not so as to touch. The young player will find this simple direction of the utmost importance; for, in the course of my experience, I have noticed many instances of failure in batters, from their ignorance of, or inattention, to this valuable rule, and who would otherwise have become very promising players. Let the learner make the trial of the two modes of holding his bat, and he will prove that when the hands are placed far apart, the one will act against the other, and that his playing will be feeble.

HOW THE BATSMAN SHOULD TAKE HIS STAND AT THE WICKET

First walk up behind the wicket, and enquire of the bowler from which side he will deliver the ball. Then take a direct view from the wicket to the place where the ball is or should be delivered. This will shew the exact spot for you to place your bat, so as to cover the middle-stump. Place your bat on this spot, upright, and make a mark in the ground in order that you may know it again. This mark is your only guide for placing your right foot at a proper distance from the wicket, behind the popping-crease. The toes should be slightly inclined towards the opposite wicket; and the left foot extended to a short distance before the popping-crease. In taking your situation at the wicket, be careful to observe that you can with ease cover the off-stump with an upright bat, and at the same time leave a clear view of the wicket to the bowler.

The young batsman should be very particular respecting his position at the wicket, since much will depend upon that. He should be able to move with ease in any direction, and place his feet, as already described, in a proper direction

B

for hitting. These should be extended only far enough to give him full power for striking. If the legs be placed too far asunder, the result will be, that he will hit *under*, instead of *over* the ball. Let him, for his own satisfaction, try the experiment of the two positions, and I have no doubt as to which he will prefer. The body also should be kept upright; it will assist him in playing well above the ball.*

HOW TO STOP A LENGTH-BALL STRAIGHT TO THE WICKET

Place the bat down, upright, on the mark made to cover the middle-stump, and the feet in their proper situation. Immediately before the ball is delivered, raise the bat steadily till you see where the ball will pitch. Then move the left foot forward, about three feet, keeping the right foot behind the popping-crease. Now move the bat as far forward as you can reach, so as to present its full face to meet the ball; keeping the bat upright, or rather slanting *the handle* towards the bowler to an angle of about 22 degrees. In order to maintain an upright position of the bat, the *left elbow* must be turned up. Let me urge the young batsman not to neglect this direction of turning up the left elbow, for he cannot play his bat upright without doing so. It is likewise the best and safest way for hitting, as well as stopping; for, if a stroke be made with the left elbow in the position stated, and the bat at the same time well upright, the ball cannot rise. I need not point out the advantage of this.

The reaching in to stop a length-ball will prevent it from rising or twisting. It will also save the hands, and, better than all, prevent the batter from being caught out. In reaching in too, be especially careful that the right foot remain firmly in place *behind* the popping-crease; for in the eagerness of playing at these balls, the foot will unconsciously draw in. Be careful therefore as to this point, for should you miss the ball, a clever wicket-keeper will surely stump you out.

* The above direction is given only with reference to the *striking*, and not the *blocking* of the ball.

I would strongly recommend the young batsman to turn his whole attention to stopping; for, by acting this part well, he becomes a serious antagonist to the bowler; who, when he sees a man coming in that he knows will stop all his length-balls with ease, he is always in a degree disheartened. He has no affection for such a customer. Besides, in this accomplishment lies the distinction between the scientific player and the random batsman.

HOW TO STOP A SHOOTING-BALL DROPPED SHORT OF A LENGTH

When you see the ball shoot, play the bat back as near to the wicket as possible, taking care not to knock it down. This backward movement will give you a better sight of the ball, and more time for stopping it. The only difficulty is to be soon enough; for, if you are not quick, the wicket will be down before your bat is.

HOW TO STOP A BALL DROPPED RATHER SHORT OF A LENGTH, AND WHICH RISES AS HIGH AS THE BAIL

This ball must also be played behind the popping-crease. The bat must be lifted from the ground high enough to play above the ball, and so as to prevent its being caught. It should also be held in the same position as when stopping a length-ball on the ground. Let me again caution the young batsman to turn up his left elbow, as he cannot well perform the motion here required without doing so. If the ball should rise higher than the wicket, let it pass, by removing your bat. My reason for giving this advice, is, that if the man, placed at the point, understand the game, he will get in close to the player while he is raising his bat; and will, in all probability, catch him out.

HOW TO PLAY AT A LENGTH-BALL A LITTLE WIDE OF THE OFF-STUMP

This is a puzzler to a short-armed batsman. I recommend the young batsman to have nothing to do with it. The old hand will, of course, do as he pleases: but I should much wish to be informed in what part of the field he can play it with safety and make a run.

BELDHAM would cut at such a ball with a horizontal bat. I once made the remark to him, that I thought it dangerous play: he answered me, 'I always play *above* the ball.' If he always played above such a ball, it was useless his playing at it at all. Now Beldham must have played from the pitch of the ball, instead of having a sight of it after it had pitched; therefore it could never be a safe hit. He was the only one of a good batter that I ever saw play at such balls.*

HOW TO PLAY AT A BALL DROPPED RATHER SHORT OF A LENGTH ON THE OFF-SIDE OF THE WICKET

There are two ways of playing at this ball, and in each I have seen it treated by the best batters.

OLD SMALL, one of the finest batsmen of his own day, or perhaps of any other, always played such balls with an *upright bat*. He would pass his left foot across the wicket, and this action gave him power and command over the ball. The upper edge of his bat was turned slightly back towards the wicket. The whole motion was performed by the wrists and arms. I never saw any batter who could use the wrist like this admirable old man.

I do not remember to have seen LAMBERT cut at a ball with the bat held horizontally: such as I have described he always played with an upright bat.

LORD BEAUCLERCK mostly, BELDHAM always, and the principal part of the best batters, play the bat horizontally at such balls.

Having now given the example of the above eminent men, some playing one way and some another, I shall venture to offer to the young batsman my own opinion. I have frequently played in both styles, and I consider holding the bat *upright* the safer, and horizontally the more *brilliant* playing. At the same time, whichever way it be

---

* Mr Ward, from his great judgement and experience, as well as from his length of limb, would play this ball gently between the middle wicket and point, and get a run.

played, I still recommend the movement of the left foot across the wicket. The power that this action gives the striker over the ball must always be felt and acknowledged.

There are other balls dropped still shorter of the length. On the off-side these may be played straight off, or between the point of the bat and the middle wicket, whichever the batsman may find most pleasant to himself; yet taking care to play well above the balls, and to hit them on the ground. In preparing and making himself up to hit a fair ball, let the batter bear in mind the sportsman's motto: 'Never to be in a flurry.' If he neglect this caution, he will surely find something wrong when it is too late to remedy it: his legs, for instance, may be too widely extended, in which case he will certainly play under the ball. More errors are committed in a man's making himself up to hit, than in the hitting: but let him prepare steadily, coolly, and with decision, and a hundred chances to one will be in favour of his hitting well. Observe any one who is batting indifferently – examine his position – see how he holds his bat, and you will rarely fail to discover in that the cause of his incompetence; for either his position will be out of rule, or his hands will be wrongly placed on the bat; and if the latter be the case, no man can strike well. Let me also strongly caution the young player against *over*-hitting, or hitting *too* hard; this will almost invariably throw him off his balance.

All straight balls should be played straight back, and with an upright bat. To cross a ball is the worst of all bad play.

HOW TO PLAY A BALL THAT IS PITCHED ON THE INSIDE OF THE LEG-STUMP SHOOTING ON THE GROUND

Draw the right foot back; play back, with the bat upright, as near to the wicket as convenient: the lower edge of the bat slightly turned towards the stumps; the wrist and arms will do the rest, if you ply them well. This is always a safe hit, and many runs are made by it. Add to which, if the batsman play these balls well, the wicket-keeper is frequently obliged to move one of the fieldsmen in, to save the run; this weakens the field, and consequently gives an advantage to the batsman.

Balls dropped short of the length on the *on*-side, or tosses, must be played on the *on*-side. The batter has but to set himself steadily to work; to take his best position – his legs right – body upright – to play above the ball, and hit it as hard as he can along the ground. I never wish to see a ball mount: for it always goes farthest when it skims like a swallow; moreover it is then safe, and, better than all, it gets the greatest number of runs. The great beauty of hitting, is to see a batsman go in and get many runs without giving a chance.

THE BEST WAY TO PLAY A BALL, BOWLED AS WIDE AS YOUR LEGS ON THE ON-SIDE

Make a quick movement in before the wicket, and hit the ball behind you. A ball played in this way is always safe, and gets many runs. It goes farther than any other, for the batter gives additional force to its speed in the direction in which it is already going. The great error in playing these balls is, that the batsman begins at them too late.

Balls tossed beyond a length must be met with a full bat, and held in the same position as when stopping a length-ball – that is, with the left elbow turned well up. The only distinction in the two cases consists in this; that on the present occasion the ball is hit; in the other, that it is blocked. Care must be taken here to strike late enough, or the ball will be hit into the bowler's hands.

If the young practitioner wish to *go in* at a *length-ball* (I speak with reference to slow bowling), it must be at a ball that comes straight to the wicket: let him bear this in mind. If the ball be wide, how can he play at it with an upright bat? and unless he do so play it, he can be at no certainty in hitting the ball: again, therefore, I repeat – the ball must be straight to the wicket; then the movement to get in must be quick; the position the same as before described. If his legs are not at their proper distance from each other, it will be impossible for him to make anything of a hit. Having pointed out the difficulty of playing these balls to advantage in this way, the learner will, of course, act as he pleases. I will, however, take the opportunity of naming the very few of the best players who have succeeded in going in at length balls. SUETER, of the Hambledon Club; HAMMOND, a Sussex man; LAMBERT, a Surrey man; and SHEARMAN,* from Mitcham. Sueter was the first player that I remember to have broken through the old rule of standing firm at the popping-crease for a length-ball. If these are the only batsmen that I remember to have succeeded upon this occasion (and I remember all the best players for fifty years back), how can the young performer expect much chance of success?

I have indeed seen others (and the finest players too) go in, and hit the ball away; but I have also seen them out by doing so; the movement, therefore, at the best is a hazardous one.

Let me conclude this department of my instructions by recapitulating the following brief mementos. *The body and bat upright – the hands near to each other – the left elbow well turned up – and the legs not too much extended.* The young batsman will find these to be golden rules for his guidance.

THE WICKET-KEEPER

holds the most important station of all the fieldsmen, and for the following reasons. He always presides at that wicket from which the ball is struck. This very circumstance will enable him to command a full view of the whole field with greater facility than any other player. His position being just behind the batsman, is another reason why his situation is the best to move the fieldsmen. He therefore is the General, and is deputed to direct all the movements of the fieldsmen: not, however, by word of command, like the military commander, but by the simple motion of his hand; and the reason for this will be obvious to every one;

* Shearman, when he has not found himself in the right position to hit such a ball, has played it softly between the middle wicket and point, and got a run.

for instead of calling out to each fieldsman distinctly, and by so doing putting the striker upon his guard, the alteration and exact position of each fieldsman is effected in perfect silence. This motion of the hand cannot, of course, be executed with effect, without the proper attention on the part of the fieldsmen; each one, therefore, upon arriving at his appointed place, should turn his eyes towards the wicket-keeper, to discover if he be satisfied with his exact position.

For instance: suppose the fieldsman to be standing out to the hip, for the purpose of saving two runs, and the wicket-keeper draw him in by a motion of his hand, to save the one run, the chance is that the striker will not be aware of this precaution on his part, and will suffer in consequence. I have frequently witnessed the advantage of this provision on the part of the wicket-keeper by the striker being out. The bowler, on the contrary, should never give any motion or signal to the fieldsmen; for being placed opposite to the striker, his intention cannot fail to be observed, and frustrated by him. He will have no difficulty in communicating his opinion to the wicket-keeper, and indeed, he may frequently have occasion to do this, for he must always have the superior advantage of noticing the capabilities of the batter, and may make his suggestions accordingly. The short-fieldsmen may also do the same; leaving the wicket-keeper, however, to the full exercise of his judgement and discretion; for no interference between the fieldsmen and wicket-keeper can ever be allowed.

The young wicket-keeper will therefore see the necessity of his knowing the exact position that each man in the field should occupy. I need not observe that slow bowling will require a very different arrangement of the field from fast bowling: in the latter case, the greater part of the field are all considerably extended.*

In short, the wicket-keeper may be considered with refer-

---

* Upon occasions of *very* fast bowling, however, the fieldsman straight off, that covers the bowler in middle wicket, is moved round to cover the middle wicket and point; and the one that covered the middle wicket and point is moved farther round to

ence to the field as the fugleman to a regiment. The duties of these others will be fully detailed when the directions are given to the fieldsmen.

The position of the wicket-keeper in his standing should be that of a man preparing to spar, so that he may in an instant move any way he pleases.

His legs should be a little extended from each other – the left forward. He should feel himself easy in his position, and ready to move in any direction. The position of the legs are of the utmost importance in this situation. The upper part of the arms, to the elbow, should hang down easily by the body. From the elbow they should incline upwards towards the chest – both hands being open – the left rather higher than the right.

The young player will do well to consider this direction as to his position, for I have known many good catches missed from an ignorance of, or inattention to, this highly important matter. The reason of it is scarcely worth detailing; for it must be obvious even to one ignorant of the game, that the man who stands with his feet close together, and hands down by his sides (like a soldier at drill), will be totally unprepared for quick action.

The wicket-keeper should also stand at a little distance behind the wicket, yet not so far back but that he may, by a short and quick step, stump out the batter should he move from his ground. My reason for recommending that he should remove a little backward from the wicket is because by his doing so the catches will be much more easy, and he may stump as well. Many wicket-keepers will frequently put down the wicket when the striker has not moved from his ground; but this practice is doubly objectionable in the eyes of a good cricketer, and is after all but a piece of stage effect, and to make a show. The more

cover the slip; and he who covered the slip is placed to cover the long-stop and the long-slip. The man straight on is often brought in to save the one run, and the long field to the hip will be brought up behind the batsman, to save the run that may be hit between the leg and the wicket.

serious wrong, however, in the action is, that it puts the striker on his guard, and prevents his getting off his ground.

The young wicket-keeper must aim to acquire the power of deciding at a glance the exact situation of every fieldsman – of those whom he wishes to stand in, for the purpose of saving one run, or out, for that of saving two.

There is only one hit the wicket-keeper should ever have to move after from the wicket: that is, when the long field to the hip is out to save the two runs, and the batsman blocks a ball between his leg and the wicket. There is no other person can save this run but the wicket-keeper, and if he wish to save it he must start before the ball is struck, or he will be too late. In this case the slip should take his place at the wicket.

If the batsmen are running, the ball should be thrown straight to the wicket, about as high as the top of the stump. The wicket-keeper should leave the wicket between himself and the ball; take the ball before the wicket, and, as he receives it, his hands should be drawn back, putting the wicket down with one motion. This should be done steadily; if it be done in a hurry it can seldom be well done.

SUETER, of the Hambledon Club, and HAMMOND, a Sussex man, were the two best wicket-keepers I ever saw. Both of them would put the wicket down without any flourishing or fuss; but I never saw either of them do so without a chance of putting out the batsman. The young wicket-keeper will do well to follow their example.

My last advice is, that the ball be always tossed easily home to the bowler.

THE POINT OF THE BAT (SLOW BOWLING)

The young fieldsman who is appointed to this situation should possess a quick eye and a quick action. Without these two qualities he will never succeed in this important place.

He should place himself within three yards and a half

of the batsman, directly opposite to the popping-crease.*
This is nearer than is generally recommended; but I have
played for many years against the best of batsmen, and
always found the distance named preferable to one farther
removed; indeed, I have more frequently played at three
yards than at three yards and a half from the batsman, and
yet never received an injury from the ball.

For the position of body in the point, I can do no
better than refer him to instructions upon this head given
to the wicket-keeper – they will be essentially the same:
the legs rather extended; arms *to* the elbows hanging easily,
and near to the body; *from* the elbow inclined upwards,
and hands open.

The next subject for this fieldsman's consideration is to
know from what balls he should play back, and at which he
should go in. Let him master this, and he need never fear
any batsman.

When the ball drops short of a length, yet straight to
the wicket, and rises, he will notice that the batsman will
be under the necessity of raising his bat high to play
above the ball. Upon such occasions he must play forward, and nearly up to the bat. By this action he will
frequently have the chance of a catch. When the batter
blocks at a length-ball, he should again play forward. If
the ball be dropped short of a length, or be tossed on
the off-side of the wicket, he will observe the batsman
preparing to hit it in the direction in which he is standing.
Before he can do this he must play back at least four
yards, and the movement must be made promptly, from the
pitch of the ball, and from the motion of the batsman
before he strikes – afterwards will be too late; besides
which he will be unable to defend himself against the ball:
the point all the while must keep his face towards the batter,
and his arms and hands in their proper position. By due
attention to this hint, he will not throw away the chance
of catching out his man. I have twice succeeded in catching

* *Autre temps, autre mœurs.* Probably the only man in the
latter half of the nineteenth century who had the courage to
stand within three yards and a half of the batsman was Mr
E. M. Grace,—Ed.

out Lord Beauclerck and many others by this movement. Independently of the advantage to be derived from playing so near, I never knew a batsman like to have the point moving in at every ball he blocked.

In backing up, this fieldsman should always keep farther from the wicket than the slip, leaving plenty of room between them.

In *fast* bowling, the station of the point should be at least seven yards from the batsman, and rather behind the popping-crease.

LONG FIELD, STRAIGHT OFF

should be an active man, and able to throw well. His station is on the off-side, between the bowler and the middle-wicket, and out far enough to save the two runs. His duty is to cover the middle wicket and bowler.

This fieldsman is occasionally brought in to save the one run.

LONG FIELD, STRAIGHT ON

should stand at some distance out from the bowler's wicket to save the two runs. When the bowling can be depended on, and the hitting is not severe, he may be brought in to save the one run.

LONG FIELD TO THE HIP*

The fieldsman must stand out to save two runs opposite to the popping-crease. Every person who takes the long-field should be able to throw well, to run well, and he should begin to run before the ball is struck: this, in the language of Cricket, is called 'getting the start of the ball.'

As in the instance of the two formerly named players, this fieldsman is frequently moved in to save the one run.

THE LONG STOP

holds a most important station in the game of cricket. His

* Square-leg—ED.

appointment is behind the wicket-keeper, and he should stand in, so as to save the one run.

When the ball does not come to his hand with a fair bound, he must go down upon his right knee with his hands before him;* then, in case these should miss it, his body will form a bulwark, and arrest its farther progress.

In addition to this duty, he is required to cover many slips from the bat, both to the leg and the off-side. It is requisite that he should learn to throw with a quick action to the top of the wicket.

SHORT SLIP

The situation for the slip is between the wicket-keeper and point of the bat, and at a rather greater distance from the wicket than the wicket-keeper, yet nearer to his side than to the point of the bat, because it affords better play for his right hand.

For the position of his body, I refer to the instructions already given to the wicket-keeper and point.

As the balls usually come from the bat to the slip with considerable swiftness, this fieldsman should be perpetually on his guard.

Whenever the wicket-keeper is compelled to leave his station, the slip should move up and supply his place till he returns.

In backing up, the slip should come next to the wicket-keeper.

THE LONG SLIP

is generally placed between the short slip and point, and near enough to save the run. I should prefer, however, his standing nearly behind the short slip, on account of the balls twisting; for, if the ball be struck to his right hand, he will surely find it twist to his left. This is a station of great difficulty in fast bowling.

* In the olden times a long stop would frequently tie a handkerchief round his right knee, in order that his dress would not become soiled when he knelt to receive the ball.—ED.

THE MIDDLE WICKET

should stand on the off-side, not more than eleven yards from the bowler's wicket, or more than twenty-two from the batsman's.

That this situation may well be filled, a person of more than common activity will be required; one who, judging from the motion of the bat, will start into action before the ball is hit; one with a quick movement of the arm in throwing, and a steady hand to return the ball into the wicket-keeper's hands at the top of the stumps. To be quick and steady are two most valuable qualifications in a fieldsman – and, indeed, in which of our worldly callings are they not valuable? There is no place in the whole field where so many struggles occur to save a run, or to put the batsman out, as at the middle wicket; add to which many catches arise, some from severe hits, others difficult to get at: with the constant movement, therefore, in covering his ground, and closely backing up, the eyes, legs, and hands of the middle wicket are never unoccupied. This situation will furnish lively employment for an active young gentleman.

LONG FIELD TO COVER THE MIDDLE WICKET AND POINT

is a situation in which the fieldsman will have many hard balls to stop, and many a one to catch. The first thing he should make himself master of is to play from the pitch of the ball, and the motion of the batsman, so as *to get the start of the ball*. By so doing he will be enabled to cover many balls that would otherwise pass him; and many catches, difficult in themselves to get at, will become comparatively easy. He must learn to judge the direction in which the batter, by his position and motion, will strike the ball, and whether high or low, hard or gently, and before it struck, he should be off to meet or cover it. This instruction will apply to either the long or the short field.

The second point of consequence to know is the exact spot where the two runs may be saved, and that where the one run may be prevented. Minute and trifling as these

matters may appear, let the young practitioner be assured
that he never will be accounted an effective fieldsman till
he have made himself master of them. Time in the play
and trouble to the wicket-keeper will be spared, and, were
no other advantage to arise, these are well worth securing.
The following, although a personal anecdote, as it bears
upon the present subject, I may be pardoned for introducing
upon this occasion. The first match of any importance in
which I played was when the Hambledon Club challenged
all England: I was then between seventeen and eighteen
years old, and played for England. The celebrated JAMES
AYLWARD was our General. His command to me was, 'You
will cover the middle wicket and point.' – 'What,' said I,
'out to save the two runs?' – 'Why, you would not play in
to save one on this ground!' – 'I would, when CLIFFORD
bowls.' (Clifford was a slow bowler.) 'You shall do as you
like,' said he, with an approving smile, and a hearty shake
of the hand. Now, the time I took to move in to save the
one run was just before the bowler had started, the batsman's eye being at that time fixed upon him. By this
manoeuvre I had the good fortune, in the course of the
match, to put out two of the Hambledon Club, and received in consequence the thanks of Sir Horace Mann.
The glory of this reward made me scarcely to know whether
I stood on my head or my heels; and, if my memory be an
honest one, some time elapsed before I had rubbed off my
conceit.

Suppose the fieldsman in this station be brought in to
save the one run—a case of frequent occurrence when the
bowling is good – he should not wait and let the ball come
to him, but dash in to meet it, fielding it with his right hand,
and, with a quick motion, throwing it at the top of the
stumps to the wicket-keeper's hands. If this act be performed neatly, it has a beautiful effect, and is the very
essence of fine fielding. It is a movement that any active
young player may attain with a little perseverance, and the
best mode of accomplishing it is to get a person to stand at
the wicket and throw the ball towards him – moderately
quick at first, increasing the speed with his improvement.

If a ball be hit very hard in the direction of the long field, the safe way to play it is by dropping on one knee with both hands before him: should these miss it, the body will act as a rampart to prevent its further progress.

To the young cricketer I cannot too frequently repeat that activity, observation, and steadiness are the most valuable qualities in a fieldsman, and allow me to add, as an old 'TUTOR' – in any other man.

SINGLE WICKET

The parties in a match at single wicket vary in number from one to six on a side. The distance between the wickets is twenty-two yards. At the bowler's wicket, two stumps are placed with a bail upon them; and this the striker, when running, must come to, and strike off, and return to his own wicket. This is counted one run. If the bail should be off, the batter must strike the stump out of the ground. When the party consists of fewer than four on each side, if the striker leave his ground to hit the ball, he will not be permitted to reckon a notch.

THE PLAY BEFORE THE WICKET

When the parties consist of fewer than five on each side, the custom of the game is, to make bounds on each side of the wicket; which bounds are to be laid down parallel with it, as well as with each other: they must likewise extend *twenty-two* yards from the wicket. The man who is in, must strike the ball before these limits, or boundary lines; and it must be returned in the same direction by those who are seeking out. It must also be thrown back in such a manner, that it may cross the play between the wicket of the batter and that of the bowler; or between the bounds and the wicket of the man who is in, before it is considered dead.

If the striker in running have knocked off the bail upon the opposite wicket and return home before the ball have struck down his wicket, or cross the play, or been between the bounds and his own wicket, it is to be considered a run.

The wicket must be put down by the ball, whether by throwing, or holding it in the hand, and always from *before*; for the ball is dead once it has been behind the wicket.

The striker may continue running so long as the ball is in play – in other words, till it has cross the play, or been returned between the bounds, or is dead in the hand of the bowler.

SINGLE WICKET WITH MORE THAN FOUR ON EACH SIDE

is subject to the same rules as when the game at double wicket, with the full complement of men, is played.

PROTEST

AGAINST THE MODERN INNOVATION OF THROWING, INSTEAD OF BOWLING THE BALLS

Having concluded my instructions to my young country-men, before I finally take my leave of them, I feel anxious to place upon record my opinion respecting a new style of playing the game of Cricket which has been adopted only within these few years. As I have not been actively engaged in the field for several seasons, my motive for offering the following observations can arise solely from a wish to preclude the possibility that my favourite amusement, while it changes in feature, should deteriorate in character.

I conceive, then, that all the fine style of hitting, which the reader will find recorded in the latter part of this little work, must in a very material degree cease, if the modern innovation of throwing, instead of bowling the ball, be not discontinued. It is not the least important objection I have to offer against the system to say, that it reduces the strikers too much to an equality; since the indifferent batsman possesses as fair a chance of success as the most refined player; and the reason for this is obvious, because, from the random manner of delivering the ball, it is impossible for the fine batsman to have time for that finesse and delicate management, which so peculiarly distinguished the elegant manoeuvring of the chief players who occupied the field about eight, ten, and more years ago. If the system continue, I freely confess that I cannot even hope again to witness such exquisite finish as distinguished the playing of such men as OLD SMALL, and AYLWARD, and the TWO WALKERS, and BELDHAM, and LORD FREDERICK BEAUCLERK: the last indeed, I believe it is pretty well understood, retired as soon as the present system was tolerated.

I am aware that the defence which has been urged in behalf of the throwing, is, that 'it tends to shorten the game'; that now a match is commonly decided in one day which heretofore occupied three times the space in its completion. This argument, I grant, is not an irrational one; but if the object in countenancing the innovation (and one, be it observed, in direct defiance of a standing law) extend solely to the 'curtailment of the game,' why not multiply the difficulties in another direction? Why not give more room for the display of skill in the batter? Why not have four stumps instead of three, and increase the length of the bails from eight inches to ten? The gentlemen forming the Mary-le-bone Club have the power to order this. Will they consider the proposal, and sanction it, seeing that the fair character of their game is at stake? And that this is actually the case I feel perfectly confident, both from my own observation and experience, as well as from the corroboration of men whose judgement I esteem. If, therefore, the present system be persisted in a few years longer, the elegant and scientific game of Cricket will decline into a mere exhibition of rough, coarse horse-play.*

I do not speak from prejudice, or from the partiality of one who has been educated in a particular school, however natural that such should be the result of my present opinion; but I can use my eyes, and I can compare notes

---

* Nyren's fears were proved by time to be quite groundless—ED.

and points in the two styles of playing; and they who have known me will bear testimony that I have never been accustomed to express myself rashly; I have, therefore, no hesitation in declaring that none of the players who have risen with the new system can compare for a moment in the standard of excellence (clever though they undoubtedly are) with the eminent men already named above, and for the reason I have assigned.

THE FIELDSMEN, AS PLACED BY NYREN FOR ORDINARY BOWLING

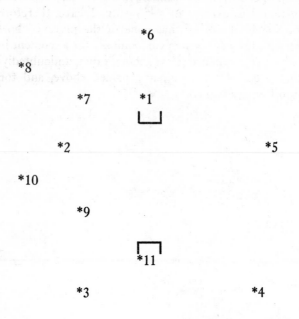

1. Wicket-keeper.
2. The Point of the Bat.
3. Long-field Straight-off.
4. Long-field Straight-on.
5. Long-field to the Hip.
6. Long-stop.
7. Short-slip.
8. The Long-slip.
9. The Middle Wicket.
10. Long-field to cover the Middle Wicket and Point.
11. The Bowler.—ED.

THE
CRICKETERS OF MY TIME

T HE game of cricket is thoroughly British. Its derivation is probably from the Saxon *cryce*, 'a stick'. Strutt, however, in his *Sports and Pastimes*, states that he can find no record of the game, under its present appellation, 'beyond the commencement of the last century, where it occurs in one of the songs published by D'Urfey'.* The first four lines of 'Of a noble race was Shenkin', ran thus:

> *'Her was the prettiest fellow*
> *At foot-ball or at* cricket
> *At hunting chase, or nimble race,*
> *How featly her could prick it.'*

The same historian of our games doubts not that cricket derived its origin from the ancient game of club-ball, the

**Pills to purge Melancholy*, 4th edit. 1719, vol. ii. p. 172.

patronymics of which being compounded of Welsh and Danish (*clwppa* and *bol*) do not warrant his conclusion, the Saxon being an elder occupant of our island. The circumstance, however, of their being no illustration extant – no missal, illuminated with a group engaged in this king of athletic games, as is the case with its plebeian brother, the club-ball; also, from its constitution, being of a more civil and complicated character – we may rationally infer that it is the offspring of a more polite, at all events, of a maturer age than its fellow. The game of club-ball appears to have been no other than the present well-known bat-and-ball, which, with similar laws and customs prescribed in the playing at it, was, doubtless, anterior to trap-ball. The trap, indeed, carries with it an air of refinement in the 'march of mechanism'.

They who are acquainted with some of the remote and unfrequented villages of England, where the primitive manners, customs, and games of our ancestors survive in the perfection of rude and unadulterated simplicity, must have remarked the lads playing at a game which is the same in its outline and principle features as the consummate piece of perfection that at this day is the glory of Lord's, and the pride of English athletæ – I mean the one in which a single stick is appointed for a wicket, ditto for a bat, and the same repeated, of about three inches in length, for a ball. If this be not the original of the game of cricket, it is a plebeian imitation of it.

My purpose, however, is not to search into the antiquities of cricketing, but to record my recollections of some of the most eminent professors of my favourite pastime who have figured on the public arena since the year 1776, when I might be about twelve years of age. From that period till within a few seasons past, I have constantly been 'at the receipt of custom' when any rousing match has been toward; and being now a veteran, and laid up in ordinary, I may be allowed the vanity of the quotation,

'Quorum magna pars fui.'*

* I learned a little Latin when I was a boy of a worthy old Jesuit, but I was a better hand at the fiddle; and many a time

I was born at Hambledon, in Hampshire – the *Attica* of
the scientific art I am celebrating. No eleven in England
could compare with the Hambledon, which met on the
first Tuesday in May on Broad-Halfpenny. So renowned
a set were the men of Hambeldon, that the whole country
round would flock to see one of their trial matches. 'Great
men', indeed, 'have been among us – better, none'; and in
the course of my recollections I shall have occasion to
instance so many within the knowledge of persons now
living, as will, I doubt not, warrant me in giving the palm
to my native place.

The two principal bowlers on my early days were
THOMAS BRETT and RICHARD NYREN, of Hambledon; the
corps de reserve, or change-bowlers, were BARBER and
HOGSFLESH. Brett was, beyond all comparison, the fastest
as well as straightest bowler that was ever known: he was
neither a thrower nor a jerker, but a legitimate downright
bowler, delivering his ball fairly, high, and very quickly,
quite as strongly as the jerkers, and with the force of a
point blank shot. He was a well-grown, dark-looking man,
remarkably strong, and with rather a short arm. As a batter,
he was comparatively an inferior player – a slashing hitter,
but he had little guard of his wicket, and his judgment of
the game was held in no great estimation. Brett, whose
occupation was that of a farmer, bore the universal character of a strictly honourable man in all his transactions,
whether in business or in amusement.

Richard Nyren was left-handed. He had a high delivery,
always to the length, and his balls were provokingly deceitful. He was the chosen General of all the matches, ordering
and directing the whole. In such esteem did the brotherhood
hold his experience and judgement, that he was uniformly
consulted on all questions of law or precedent; and I never
knew an exception to be taken against his opinion, or his
decision to be reversed. I never saw a finer specimen
of the thoroughbred old English yeoman than Richard

have I taught the gipseys a tune during their annual visits to
our village, thereby purchasing the security of our poultry-
yard. When the hand of the destroyer was stretched forth over
the neighbouring roosts, our little Goshen was always passed by.

Nyren. He was a good face-to-face, unflinching, uncompromising, independent man. He placed a full and just value
upon the station he held in society, and he maintained it
without insolence or assumption. He could differ with a
superior, without trenching upon his dignity, or losing his
own. I have known him maintain an opinion with great
firmness against the Duke of Dorset and Sir Horace Mann;
and when, in consequence of his being proved to be in the
right, the latter has afterwards crossed the ground and
shaken him heartily by the hand. Nyren had immense
advantage over Brett; for independently of his general
knowledge of the game, he was practically a better cricketer,
being a safe batsman and an excellent hitter. Although a very
stout man (standing about five feet nine) he was uncommonly active. He owed all the skill and judgement he
possessed to an old uncle, Richard Newland, of Slindon, in
Sussex, under whom he was brought up – a man so famous
in his time, that when a song was written in honour of the
Sussex cricketers, Richard Newland was especially and
honourably signalised. No one man ever dared to play him.
When Richard Nyren left Hambledon, the club broke up,
and never resumed from that day. The head and right arm
were gone.

Barber and Hogsflesh were both good hands; they had a
high delivery, and a generally good length; not very strong,
however, at least for those days of playing, when the bowling
was all fast. These four were our tip-top men, and I think
such another stud was not to be matched in the whole
kingdom, either before or since. They were choice fellows,
staunch and thorough-going. No thought of treachery ever
seemed to have entered their heads. The modern politics of
trickery and 'crossing' were (so far as my own experience
and judgement of their actions extended) as yet 'a sealed
book' to the Hambledonians; what they did, they did for
the love of honour and victory; and when one (who shall be
nameless) sold the birthright of his good name for a mess
of pottage, he paid dearly for his bargain. It cost him the
trouble of being a knave – (no trifle!); the esteem of his old
friends, and, what was worst of all, the respect of him who
could have been his *best* friend – himself.

Upon coming to the old batters of our club, the name of JOHN SMALL, the elder, shines among them in all the lustre of a star of the first magnitude. His merits have already been recorded in a separate publication, which every zealous brother of the pastime has probably read. I need, therefore, only subscribe my testimony to his uncommon talent, shortly summing up his chief excellences. He was the best short runner of his day, and indeed I believe him to have been the first who turned the short hits to account. His decision was as prompt as his eye was accurate in calculating a short run. Add to the value of his accomplishment as a batter, he was an admirable fieldsman, always playing middle wicket; and so correct was his judgement of the game, that old Nyren would appeal to him when a point of law was being debated. Small was a remarkably well-made and well-knit man, of honest expression, and as active as a hare.

He was a good fiddler, and taught himself the double bass. The Duke of Dorset having been informed of his musical talent, sent him as a present a handsome violin, and paid the carriage. Small, like a true and simple-hearted Englishman, returned the compliment, by sending his Grace two bats and balls, also *paying the carriage*. We may be sure that on both hands the presents were choice of their kind. Upon one occasion he turned his Orphean accomplishment to good account. Having to cross two or three fields on his way to a musical party, a vicious bull made at him; when our hero, with the characteristic coolness and presence of mind of a good cricketer, began playing upon his bass, to the admiration and perfect satisfaction of the mischievous beast.

About this time, 1778, I became a sort of farmer's pony to my native club of Hambledon, and I never had cause to repent the work I was put to; I gained by it that various knowledge of the game which I leave in the hands of those who knew me in my 'high and palmy state' to speak to and appreciate. This trifling preliminary being settled, the name and figure of TOM SUETER first comes across me – a Hambledon man, and of the club. What a handful of steel-hearted soldiers are in an important pass, such was Tom in keeping the wicket. Nothing went by him; and for coolness and nerve in this trying and responsible post, I never saw his equal. As a proof of his quickness and skill, I have numberless times seen him stump a man out with Brett's tremendous bowling. Add to this valuable accomplishment, he was one of the manliest and most graceful of hitters. Few would cut a ball harder at the point of the bat, and he was, moreover, an excellent short runner. He had an eye like an eagle – rapid and comprehensive. He was the first who departed from the custom of the old players before him, who deemed it a heresy to leave the crease for the ball; he would get in at it, and hit it straight off and straight on; and, egad! it went as if it had been fired. As by the rules of our club, at the trial-matches no man was allowed to get more than thirty runs, he generally gained his number earlier than any of them. I have seldom seen a handsomer man than Tom Sueter, who measured about five feet ten. As if, too, Dame Nature wished to show at his birth a specimen of her prodigality, she gave him so amiable a disposition, that he was the pet of all the neighbourhood: so honourable a heart, that his word was never questioned by the gentlemen who associated with him: and a voice, which for sweetness, power, and purity of tone (a tenor), would, with proper cultivation, have made him a handsome fortune. With what rapture have I hung upon his notes when he has given us a hunting song in the club-room after the day's practice was over!

GEORGE LEER, of Hambledon, who always answered to the title among us of 'Little George', was our best long-stop. So firm and steady was he, that I have known him stand through a whole match against Brett's bowling, and not lose more than two runs. The ball seemed to go into him, and he was as sure of it as if he had been a sand-bank. His activity was so great, and, besides, he had so good a judgement in running to cover the ball, that he would stop many that were hit in the slip, and this, be it remembered, from the swiftest bowling ever known. The portion of ground that man would cover was quite extraordinary. He was a good batsman, and a tolerably sure guard of his wicket; he averaged from fifteen to twenty runs, but I

never remember his having a long innings. What he did
not bring to the stock by his bat, however, he amply made
up with his perfect fielding. Leer was a short man, of a fair
complexion, well-looking, and of a pleasing aspect. He had
a sweet counter-tenor voice. Many a treat have I had in
hearing him and Sueter join in a glee at the 'Bat and Ball'
on Broad-Halfpenny:

> 'I have been there, and still would go;
> 'Twas like a little heaven below!'

EDWARD ABURROW, a native of Hambledon, was one of
our best long fields. He always went by the name of Curry;
why, I cannot remember, neither is it of the utmost importance to enquire. He was well calculated for the post he
always occupied, being a sure and strong thrower, and able
to cover a great space of the field. He was a steady and safe
batter, averaging the same number of runs as Leer. We
reckoned him a tolerably good change for bowling.
Aburrow was a strong and well-made man, standing
about five feet nine; he had a plain, honest-looking face,
and was beloved by all his acquaintance.

BUCK, whose real name was PETER STEWART, is the next
Hambledon man that occurs to my recollection. He, too,
played long field, and was a steady man at his post; his
batting, too, reached the same pitch of excellence; he could
cut the balls very hard at the point of the bat – nothing like
Sueter, however – very few could have equalled *him*. Buck
was a dark-looking man, a shoemaker by trade, in height
about five feet eight, rather slimly built, and very active.
He had an ambition to be thought a humorist. The following
anecdote may serve both as a specimen of his talent, and of
the unfastidious taste of the men of Hambledon. When a
match was to be played at a distance, the whole eleven, with
the umpire and scorer, were conveyed in one caravan, built
for their accommodation. Upon one occasion, the vehicle
having been overturned, and the whole cargo unshipped,
Buck remained at his post, and refused to come out, desiring
that they would right the vessel with him in it; for that 'one
good turn deserved another'. This repartee was admired for
a week.

The following old-fashioned song, and which was very popular fifty years ago, may bring back pleasant recollections to those of my countrymen who remember the Hambledon Club in the year 1778.

CRICKET

BY THE REV MR COTTON, OF WINCHESTER.

Assist, all ye Muses, and join to rehearse
An old English sport, never praised yet in verse:
'Tis Cricket I sing, of illustrious fame,
No nation e'er boasted so noble a game.
      Derry down, &c.

Great Pindar has bragg'd of his heroes of old –
Some were swift in the race, some in battles were bold;
The brows of the victor with olives were crown'd:
Hark! they shout, and Olympia returns the glad sound!
      Derry down, &c.

What boasting of Castor and Pollux's brother –
The one famed for riding, for boxing the other;
Compared with our heroes, they'll not shine at all –
What were Castor and Pollux to Nyren and Small?
      Derry down, &c.

Here's guarding and catching, and throwing and tossing,
And bowling and striking, and running and crossing;
Each mate must excel in some principal part –
The Pentathlum of Greece could not show so much art.
      Derry down, &c.

The parties are met, and array'd all in white –
Famed Elis ne'er boasted so pleasing a sight;
Each nymph looks askew at his favourite swain,
And views him, half stript, both with pleasure and pain.
      Derry down, &c.

The wickets are pitched now, and measured the
    ground;
Then they form a large ring, and stand gazing around –
Since Ajax fought Hector, in sight of all Troy,
No contest was seen with such fear and such joy.
    Derry down, &c.

Ye bowlers, take heed, to my precepts attend:
On you the whole fate of the game must depend;
Spare your vigour at first, now exert all your strength,
But measure each step, and be sure pitch a length.
    Derry down, &c.

Ye fieldsmen, look sharp, lest your pains ye beguile
Move close like an army, in rank and in file;
When the ball is returned, back it sure, for I trow,
Whole states have been ruined by one overthrow.
    Derry down, &c.

Ye strikers, observe when the foe shall draw nigh;
Mark the bowler, advancing with vigilant eye;
Your skill all depends upon distance and sight,
Stand firm to your scratch, let your bat be upright.
    Derry down, &c.

And now the game's o'er, IO victory! rings,
Echo doubles her chorus, and Fame spread her wings;
Let's now hail our champions all steady and true,
Such as Homer ne'er sung of, nor Pindar e'er knew.
    Derry down, &c.

Buck, Curry, and Hogsflesh, and Barber and Brett,
Whose swiftness in bowling was ne'er equalled yet;
I had almost forgot, they deserve a large bumper;
Little George, the long-stop, and Tom Sueter, the
    stumper.
    Derry down, &c.

Then why should we fear either Sackville or Mann,
Or rapine at the loss both of Boynton and Lann? –
With such troops as those we'll be lords of the game,
Spite of Minshull and Miller, and Lumpy and Frame.
    Derry down, &c.

Then fill up your glass, he's the best that drinks most.
Here's the Hambledon Club! – who refuses the toast?
Let's join in the praise of the bat and the wicket,
And sing in full chorus the patrons of cricket.
    Derry down, &c.

And when the game's o'er, and our fate shall draw nigh
(For the heroes of cricket, like others, must die),
Our bats we'll resign, neither troubled nor vex'd,
And give up our wickets to those that come next.
    Derry down, &c.

The tenth knight of our round table (of which old Richard
Nyren was the King Arthur), was a man we always called
'The Little Farmer'; his name was LAMBORN. He was a
bowler – right-handed, and he had the most extraordinary
delivery I ever saw. The ball was delivered quite low, and
with a twist; not like that of the generality of right-handed
bowlers, but just the reverse way: that is, if bowling to a
right-handed hitter, his ball would twist from the off-stump
into the leg. He was the first I remember who introduced
this deceitful and teasing style of delivering the ball. When
all England played the Hambledon Club, the Little Farmer
was appointed one of our bowlers; and, egad! this new
trick of his so bothered the Kent and Surrey men, that they
tumbled out one after another, as if they had been picked
off by a rifle corps. For a long time they could not tell
what to make of that cursed twist of his. This, however,
was the only virtue he possessed, as a cricketer. He was no
batter, and had no judgement of the game. The perfection
he had attained in this one department, and his otherwise
general deficiency, are at once accounted for by the circumstance, that when he was tending his father's sheep,
he would set up a hurdle or two, and bowl away for hours

together. Our General, old Nyren, after a great deal of trouble (for the Farmer's comprehension did not equal the speed of lightning), got him to pitch the ball a little to the off-side of the wicket, when it would twist full in upon the stumps. Before he had got into this knack, he was once bowling against the Duke of Dorset, and, delivering his ball straight to the wicket, it curled in, and missed the Duke's leg-stump by a hair's-breadth. The plain-spoken little bumpkin, in his eagerness and delight, and forgetting the style in which we were always accustomed to impress our aristocratical playmates with our acknowledgement of their rank and station, bawled out – 'Ah! it was *tedious* near you, Sir!' The familiarity of his tone, and the genuine Hampshire dialect in which it was spoken, set the whole ground laughing. I have never seen but one *bowler* who delivered his balls in the same way as our Little Farmer; with the *jerkers* the practice is not uncommon. He was a very civil and inoffensive young fellow, and remained in the club perhaps two or three seasons.

With TOM TAYLOR the old *eleven* was completed. There were of course, several changes of other players, but these were the established picked set – the *élite*. Tom was an admirable field – certainly one of the very finest I ever saw. His station was between the point of the bat and the middle wicket, to save the two runs; but Tom had a lucky knack of gathering in to the wicket, for Tom had a licence from our old General; so that, if the ball was hit to him, he had so quick a way of meeting it, and with such a rapid return (for no sooner was it in his hand, than with the quickness of thought it was returned to the top of the wicket), that I have seen many put out by this manœuvre in a single run, and when the hit might be safely calculated upon for a prosperous one. He had an excellent general knowledge of the game; but of fielding, in particular, he was perfect both in judgement and practice. Tom was also a most brilliant hitter, but his great fault lay in not sufficiently guarding his wicket: he was too fond of cutting, at the point of the bat, balls that were delivered straight; although therefore, he would frequently get many runs, yet from this habit, he could not be securely depended on; and, indeed, it was commonly the cause of his being out. I have known Lord Frederick Beauclerck (certainly the finest batter of his day) throw away the chance of a capital innings by the same incaution – that of cutting at *straight* balls, and he has been bowled out in consequence. Taylor was a short, well-made man, strong, and as watchful and active as a cat; but in no other instance will the comparison hold good, for he was without guile, and was an attached friend.

Having now described the best of my native players, I proceed to their opponents; and the foremost man of all must stand the well-known bowler, LUMPY, whose real name was STEVENS. He was a Surrey man, and lived with Lord Tankerville. Beyond all the men within my recollection, Lumpy would bowl the greatest number of length balls in succession. His pace was much faster than Lord Beauclerck's, but he wanted his Lordship's general knowledge of the game. In those days it was the custom for the party going from home to pitch their own wickets; and here it was that Lumpy, whose duty it was to attend to this, always committed an error. He would invariably choose the ground where his balls would *shoot*, instead of selecting a rising spot to bowl against, which would have materially increased the difficulty to the hitter, seeing that so many more would be caught out by the mounting of the ball. As nothing, however, delighted the old man like bowling a wicket down with a shooting ball, he would sacrifice the other chances to the glory of that achievement. Many a time have I seen our General twig this prejudice in the old man when matched against us, and chuckle at it. But I believe it was almost the only mistake he ever made professional, or even moral, for he was a most simple and amiable creature. Yes – one other he committed, and many a day after was the joke remembered against him. One of our matches having been concluded early in the day, a long, raw-boned devil of a countryman came up, and offered to play any one of the twenty-one at single wicket for five pounds. Old Nyren told Lumpy it would be five pounds easily earned, and persuaded him to accept the challenge. Lumpy, however, would not stake the whole sum himself, but offered a pound of the money, and the rest was subscribed. The confident old bowler made the countryman go in first, for he thought to settle his business in a twink; but the fellow having an arm as long as a hop-pole, reached in at Lumpy's balls, bowl what length he might; and slashed and thrashed away in the most ludicrous style, hitting his balls all over the field, and always up in the air; and he made an uncommon number of runs from this prince of bowlers before he could get him out; – and egad! he beat him! – for when Lumpy went in, not being a good batter, while the other was a very fast bowler, all along the ground, and straight to the wicket, he knocked him out presently: the whole ring roaring with laughter, and the astounded old bowler swearing he would never play another single match as long as he lived – an oath, I am sure, he religiously observed, for he was confoundedly crestfallen. Lumpy was a short man, round-shouldered, and stout. He had no trick about him, but was as plain as a pike-staff in all his dealings.

FRAME was the other principal with Lumpy; a fast bowler, and an unusually stout man for a cricketer. I recollect very little of him, and nothing worthy of a formal record.

Besides him there was SHOCK WHITE, another bowler on the England side; a good change, and a very decent hitter; but take him altogether, I never thought very highly of his playing. He was a short and rather stoutly-made man.

JOHN WOOD made the fourth, and the other change bowler. He was tall, stout, and bony, and a very good general player; not, however, an extraordinary one, when compared with those that have been heretofore mentioned.

There was high feasting held on Broad-Halfpenny during the solemnity of one of our grand matches. Oh! it was a heart-stirring sight to witness the multitude forming a complete and dense circle round that noble green. Half the county would be present, and all their hearts with us – Little Hambledon, pitted against all England was a proud thought for the Hampshire men. Defeat was glory in such a struggle – victory, indeed, made us only 'a little lower than angels'. How these fine brawn-faced fellows of farmers would drink to our success! And then, what stuff they had

C

to drink! – Punch! – not your new *Ponche à la Romaine*, or *Ponche à la Groseille*, or your modern cat-lap milk punch – punch be-deviled; but good, unsophisticated John Bull stuff, – stark! – that would stand on end – punch that would make a cat speak! Sixpence a bottle! We had not sixty millions of interest to pay in those days. The ale too! – not the modern horror under the same name that drives as many men melancholy-mad as the hypocrites do; – not the beastliness of these days, that will make a fellow's inside like a shaking bog – and as rotten; but barley-corn, such as would put the souls of three butchers into one weaver. Ale that would flare like turpentine – genuine Boniface! – This immortal viand (for it was more than liquor) was vended at twopence per pint. The immeasurable villainy of our vintners would, with their march of intellect (if ever they could get such a brewing), drive a pint of it out into a gallon. Then the quantity the fellows would eat! Two or three of them would strike dismay into a round of beef. They could no more have pecked in that style than they could have flown, had the infernal black stream (that type of Acheron!) which soddens the carcass of a Londoner, been the fertiliser of their clay. There would this company, consisting most likely of some thousands, remain patiently and anxiously watching every turn of fate in the game, as if the event had been the meeting of two armies to decide their liberty. And whenever a Hambledon man made a good hit, worth four or five runs, you would hear the deep mouths of the whole multitude baying away in pure Hampshire – 'Go hard! – go hard! – *Tich* and turn! – *tich* and turn!' To the honour of my countrymen, let me bear testimony upon this occasion also, as I have already done upon others. Although their provinciality in general, and personal partialities individually, were naturally interested in behalf of the Hambledon men, I cannot call to recollection an instance of their wilfully stopping a ball that had been hit out among them by one of our opponents. Like *true* Englishmen, they would give an enemy fair play. How strongly are all those scenes, of fifty years bygone, painted in my memory! – and the smell of that ale comes upon me as freshly as the new May flowers.

Having premised that these grand matches were always made for £500 a side, I now proceed with a slight record of the principal men who were usually pitted against us. My description of them must unavoidably be less minute, because I had not so frequent an intercourse with them as with the men whose every action I was constantly in the habit of watching: my report of them, therefore, may be more slight than their merits deserve, for there were really some fine players among them. For the same reason also, my chronicle will be less relieved by personal anecdote.

My last account having closed with the four principal bowlers who were usually opposed to us – Lumpy and Frame, Shock White and Wood – the next name that presents itself to me is that of MINSHULL, who was a gardener to the Duke of Dorset. He was a batter, and a very fine one – probably their best; a capital hitter, and a sure guard of his wicket. Minshull, however, was not an elegant player; his position and general style were both awkward and uncouth; yet he was as conceited as a wagtail, and from his constantly aping what he had no pretensions to, was on that account only, not estimated according to the price at which he had rated his own merits. He was a thick-set man, standing about five feet nine, and not very active.

MILLER (gamekeeper either to Lord Tankerville or the Duke of Dorset, I forget which) was as amiable a hearted man as ever cut a ball at the point of the bat. He and Minshull were the only two batters the Hambledon men were afraid of. Miller was indeed a beautiful player, and always to be depended on; there was no flash – no cock-a-whoop about him, but firm he was, and steady as the Pyramids. Although fully as stout a man as Minshull, he was considerably more active. I remember when upon one occasion those two men, being in together, had gained an uncommon number of runs, the backers of the Hambledon men, Dehaney and Paulet, began to quake, and edged off all their money, laying it pretty thickly on the England side. Of the Hambledon men, Small went in first, and continued until there were about five out, for very few runs, when Nyren went in to him; and then they began to show fight. The mettle of our true blood was roused into full action,

c*

and never did they exhibit to finer advantage. Nyren got 98, and Small 110 runs before they were parted. After the former was out (for Small, according to his custom, died a natural death) the backers came up to Nyren and said, 'You will win the match, and we shall lose our money'. The proud old yeoman turned short upon them, and, with that honest independence which gained him the esteem of all parties, told them to their heads that they were rightly served, and that he was glad of it. 'Another time' (said he) 'don't bet your money against such men as we are!' I forget how many runs the Hambledon men got, but, after this turn in affairs, the others stood no chance, and were easily beaten.

MAY and BROOKER, and QUIDDINGTON, were players of the first rank, though not the first of that rank. They were excellent and steady batters, strong hitters, and sure fields. Quiddington was a long-stop, and an admirable one; not, however, so implicitly to be depended on as Leer, whose equal in that department of the game I never saw anywhere. My reason for assigning him this superiority has been already given. For the same cause, too, I must place our Sueter above Yalden, who was their best wicket-keeper, and he would have been highly prized anywhere; but neither he nor Quiddington ever had to stand against such steam-engine bowling as Brett's; and yet Leer and Sueter, in their several departments, were safer men than their opponents. Yalden, too, was in other respects an inferior man to Sueter. His word was not always to be depended on when he had put a man out – he would now and then shuffle, and resort to trick. In such estimation did the other stand with all parties, so high an opinion had they of his honour – that I firmly believe they would have trusted to his decision, had he ever chosen to question that of the umpire. Yalden was not a fine, but a very useful and steady batter. He was a thin, dark-looking man.

THE DUKE OF DORSET, or LORD TANKERVILLE, sometimes both, would play, to complete the eleven. Neither of these noblemen was to be compared to Lord Frederick Beau-clerck. Whether in batting, bowling, or indeed in any department of the game, he would have distanced them;

yet they were pretty players. Each usually played in the slip when the other was not present. This station was the Duke's *forte*. He was in height about five feet nine, very well made, and had a peculiar habit, when unemployed, of standing with his head on one side.

About the period I have been describing, NOAH MANN joined the Hambledon Club. He was from Sussex, and lived at North Chapel, not far from Petworth. He kept an inn there, and used to come a distance of at least twenty miles every Tuesday to practise. He was a fellow of extraordinary activity, and could perform clever feats of agility on horseback. For instance, when he has been seen in the distance coming up the ground, one or more of his companions would throw down handkerchiefs, and these he would collect, stooping from his horse while it was going at full speed. He was a fine batter, a fine field, and the swiftest runner I ever remember: indeed, such was his fame for speed, that whenever there was a match going forward, we were sure to hear of one being made for Mann to run against some noted competitor; and such would come from the whole country round. Upon these occasions he used to tell his friends, 'If when we are half-way, you see me alongside of my man, you may always bet your money upon me, for I am sure to win'. And I never saw him beaten. He was a most valuable fellow in the field; for besides being very sure of the ball, his activity was so extraordinary that he would dart all over the ground like lightning. In those days of fast bowling, they would put a man behind the long-stop, that he might cover both long-stop and slip: the man always selected for this post was Noah. Now and then little George Leer (whom I have already described as being so fine a long-stop), would give Noah the wink to be on his guard, who would gather close behind him: then George would make a slip on purpose, and let the ball go by, when, in an instant, Noah would have it up, and into the wicket-keeper's hands, and the man was put out. This I have seen done many times, and this nothing but the most accomplished skill in fielding could have achieved.

Mann would, upon occasion, be employed as a change-bowler, and in this department he was very extraordinary.

He was left-handed, both as bowler and batter. In the former quality, his merit consisted in giving a curve to the ball the whole way. In itself it was not the first-rate style of bowling, but so very deceptive, that the chief end was frequently attained. They who remember the dexterous manner with which the Indian jugglers communicated the curve to the balls they spun round their heads, by a twist of the wrist or hand, will at once comprehend Noah's curious feat in bowling. Sometimes when a batter had got into his hitting, and was scoring more runs than pleased our General, he would put Mann in to give him eight or twelve balls, and he almost always did so with good effect.

Noah was a good batsman, and a most severe hitter; by the way, I have observed this to be a common quality in left-handed men. The writer of this was in with him at a match on Windmill-down, when by one stroke from a toss that he hit behind him, we got ten runs. At this time the playing-ground was changed from Broad-Halfpenny to the above-named spot, at the suggestion of the Duke of Dorset and the other gentlemen, who complained of the bleakness of the old place. The alteration was in this, as in every other respect, for the better, Windmill-down being one of the finest places for playing on I ever saw. The ground gradually declined every way from the centre: the fieldsmen therefore were compelled to look about them, and for this reason they became so renowned in that department of the game.

At a match of the Hambledon Club against all England, the club had to go in to get the runs, and there was a long number of them. It became quite apparent that the game would be closely fought. Mann kept on worrying old Nyren to let him go in, and although he became quite indignant at his constant refusal, our General knew what he was about in keeping him back. At length, when the last but one was out, he sent Mann in, and there were then ten runs to get. The sensation now all over the ground was greater than anything of the kind I ever witnessed before or since. All knew the state of the game, and many thousands were hanging upon this narrow point. There was Sir Horace Mann, walking about, outside the ground, cutting down the daisies with his stick – a habit with him when he was agitated; the old farmers leaning forward upon their tall old staves, and the whole multitude perfectly still. After Noah had had one or two balls. Lumpy tossed one a little too far, when our fellow got in, and hit it out in his grand style. Six of the ten were gained. Never shall I forget the roar that followed this hit. Then there was a dead stand for some time, and no runs were made; ultimately, however, he gained them all, and won the game. After he was out, he upbraided Nyren for not putting him in earlier. 'If you had let me go in an hour ago' (said he), 'I would have served them in the same way.' But the old tactician was right, for he knew Noah to be a man of such nerve and self-posses-sion, that the thought of so much depending upon him would not have the paralysing effect that it would upon many others. He was sure of him, and Noah afterwards felt the compliment. Mann was short in stature, and, when stripped, as swarthy as a gipsy. He was all muscle, with no incumbrance whatever of flesh; remarkably broad in the chest, with large hips and spider legs; he had not an ounce of flesh about him, but it was where it ought to be. He always played without his hat (the sun could not affect *his* complexion), and he took a liking to me as a boy, because I did the same. Poor Noah! his death was a very deplor-able one. Having been out shooting all day with some friends, they finished their evening with a free carouse, and he could not be persuaded to go to bed, but persisted in sleeping all night in his chair in the chimney-corner. It was, and still is, the custom in that part of the country, to heap together all the ashes on the hearth for the purpose of keeping the fire in till the next day. During the night my poor playmate fell upon the embers, and being unable to help himself, burned his side so severely that he did not survive twenty-four hours.

RICHARD FRANCIS was a Surrey man. One day I met him in the street of Hambledon, and ran to tell our General that the famous Francis had come to live among us; he could scarcely believe me – perhaps for joy. This was the luckiest thing that could have happened for us, for Brett had just about the same time left off playing.

Francis was a fast *jerker*; but though his delivery was allowed to be fair bowling, still it was a jerk. We enlisted him immediately, for we all knew what he could do, having seen him play on the Surrey side against us. At that time he was a young man, and he remained many years in the club. He was a gamekeeper; a closely-made, firm little man, and active. His batting did not deserve any marked praise, still we always set him down for a few runs. He was both a better batter, however, and field too, than Brett; but as a bowler, he ranked many degrees below that fine player.

About the same period RICHARD PURCHASE joined us. He was a slowish bowler – rather faster than Lord Beauclerk. His balls got uncommonly well, and they were generally to a length. But he had no cunning about him; nor was he up to the tricks of the game – in playing, as in all other actions in life, he was the same straightforward honest fellow. Purchase was a fair hitter,* and a tolerably good field. He was a slightly-made man, and of a dark complexion.

At this great distance from the period at which my recollection of cricketing commenced, and having no data by which to regulate them, the reader will good-naturedly make allowance both for the desultory character of my records, their unfinished and hasty sketchiness, and also for my now and then retracing my steps, to include some circumstance which, at the time of writing, had escaped my memory. For instance, I should have chronicled the era when the old-fashioned wicket of *two* stumps was changed to *three* – a decided improvement, seeing that it multiplied the chances to the batter of being bowled out, consequently increased the difficulty of his position, and thereby exalted his maintaining it for any length of time into the greater merit; for, under the old system, if the ball passed between the stumps, the batter was not considered out; under the

---

* Purchase and William Harding, of Frensham, once went in first in the second innings of a match for 228 runs. They obtained two hundred before being parted, but all the other players made only twenty more between them, thus losing the match. This startling collapse occurred at a time when betting on results was the rule rather than the exception—ED.

improved system, such an event cannot happen, for the three stumps are not pitched at so great a distance from each other as to allow of the transit of the ball without knocking off the bail. This explanation is, of course, addressed only to the young and inexperienced player. The important reform in the game here alluded to took place, according to the best of my recollection, about the year 1779 or 1780. Since that time other entrenchments have been made upon the old constitution, which was the pride of our ancestors and the admiration of the whole community; but which, so far from contributing to its stability, will, in my opinion, if not retrieved, not only essentially change, but even destroy its character; let the patrician legislators and guardians of cricket-law look to it.

Before I proceed with my catalogue of the Hambledon Pantheon, it may be worth while to mention a circumstance connected with poor Noah Mann, the player named a few pages back. As it will tend to show the amenity in which the men of lower grade in society lived in those good old times with their superiors, it may prove no worthless example to the more aristocratic, and certainly less beloved members of the same rank in society of the present day. Poor Noah was very ambitious that his new-born son should bear the Christian name, with the sanction of his namesake, Sir Horace Mann. Old Nyren, who, being the link between the patricians and plebeians in our community – the *juste milieu* – was always applied to in cases of similar emergency, undertook, upon the present occasion, to bear the petition of Noah to Sir Horace, who, with a winning condescension, acceded to the worthy fellow's request, and consented to become godfather to the child, giving it his own name; adding, I have no doubt, a present suited to the station of his little protégé. How easy a thing it is to win the esteem of our inferiors; and how well worth the while, when the mutual pleasure only, resulting from the action, is considered! Sir Horace, by this simple act of graceful humanity, hooked for life the heart of poor Noah Mann; and in this world of hatred and contention, the love even of a dog is worth living for.

The next player I shall name is JAMES AYLWARD. His

father was a farmer. After he had played with the club for a few years, Sir Horace got him away from us, and made him his bailiff, I think, or some such officer; I remember, however, he was but ill qualified for his post. Aylward was a left-handed batter, and one of the safest hitters I ever knew in the club. He once stayed in two whole days, and upon that occasion got the highest number of runs that had ever been gained by any member – *one hundred and sixty-seven*! Jemmy was not a good fieldsman, neither was he remarkably active. After he had left us, to go down to live with Sir Horace, he played against us, but never to my recollection, with any advantage to his new associates – the Hambledonians were almost always too strong for their opponents. He was introduced to the club by Tom Taylor, and Tom's anxiety upon the occasion, that his friend should do credit to his recommendation, was curiously conspicuous. Aylward was a stout,* well-made man, standing about five feet nine inches; not very light about the limbs, indeed he was rather clumsy. He would sometimes affect a little grandeur of manner, and once got laughed at by the whole ground for calling for a lemon to be brought to him when he had been in but a little while. It was thought a piece of finnickiness by those simple and homely yeomen.

And now for those anointed clod-stumpers, the WALKERS, TOM and HARRY. Never sure came two such unadulterated rustics into a civilised community. How strongly are the figures of the men (of Tom's in particular) brought to my mind when they first presented themselves to the club, upon Windmill-down. Tom's hard, ungain, scrag-of-mutton frame; wilted, apple-john face (he always looked twenty years older than he really was), his long spider legs, as thick at the ankles as at the hips, and

---

* Most of the old players appear to have been corpulent (see *Surrey Cricket: Its History and Associations.* London: Longmans, 1902, p. 37). Almost all the cricketers mentioned by Nyren, with the exceptions of Noah Mann and Scott, reached great ages. Especially was this the case with John Small, sen. (89), William Beldham (96), Aylward (86), Purchase (80), Aburrow (88), 'Shock' White (91), Lumpy (84), and Yalden (84) —ED.

perfectly straight all the way down – for the embellish-
ment of a calf in Tom's leg, Dame Nature had considered
would be but a wanton superfluity. Tom was the driest and
most rigid-limbed chap I ever knew; his skin was like the
rind of an old oak, and as sapless. I have seen his knuckles
handsomely knocked about from Harris's bowling; but never
saw any blood upon his hands – you might just as well
attempt to phlebotomise a mummy.* This rigidity of muscle
(or rather I should say of tendon for muscle was another
ingredient economised in the process of Tom's configura-
tion) – this rigidity, I say, was carried into every motion. He
moved like the rude machinery of a steam-engine in the
infancy of construction, and when he ran, every member
seemed ready to fly to the four winds. He toiled like a tar
on horseback. The uncouth actions of these men furnished
us, who prided ourselves upon a certain grace in movement
and finished air, with an ever-lasting fund of amusement,
and for some time they took no great fancy to me, because
I used to worry, and tell them they could not play. They
were, however, good hands when they first came among
us, and had evidently received most excellent instruction;
but after they had derived the advantage of first-rate practice, they became most admirable batters, and were the
trustiest fellows (particularly Tom) in cases of emergency
or difficulty. They were devilish troublesome customers to
get out. I have very frequently known Tom to go in first
and remain to the very last man. He was the coolest, the
most imperturbable fellow in existence: it used to be said
of him that he had no nerves at all. Whether he was only
practising, or whether he knew that the game was in a
critical state, and that much depended upon his play,
he was the same phlegmatic, unmoved man – he was the
Washington of cricketers. Neither he nor his brother was
active, yet both were effective fieldsmen. Upon one occasion,
on the Mary-le-bone grounds, I remember Tom going in
first, and Lord Frederick Beauclerck giving him the first

* Beldham, in Pycroft's *Cricket Field*, gives Nyren the lie. 'I
have seen Tom Walker,' he says, 'rub his bleeding fingers in the
dust! David Harris used to say he liked to *rind* him'—ED.

four balls all of an excellent length. First four or last four made no difference to Tom – he was always the same cool, collected fellow. Every ball he dropped down just before his bat. Off went his lordship's white hat – dash upon the ground (his constant action when disappointed) – calling him at the same time 'a confounded old beast.' – 'I doan't care what ee zays,' said Tom when one close by asked if he had heard Lord Frederick call him 'an old beast.' No, no; Tom was not the man to be flustered.

About a couple of years after Walker had been with us, he began the system of throwing instead of bowling, now so much the fashion. At that time it was esteemed foul play, and so it was decided by a council of the Hambledon Club, which was called for the purpose. The first I recollect seeing revive the custom was Willes, a Sussex man. I am decidedly of the opinion, that if it be not stopped altogether, the character of the game will become changed. I should hope that such powerful and efficient members of the Mary-le-bone Club, as Mr Ward &c. will determine, not only to discountenance, but wholly and finally to suppress it; and instead, to foster and give every encouragement to genuine, *bonâ fide* bowlers – men with a fine delivery.

I never thought much of Tom's bowling; indeed the bowling of that time was so supereminent, that he was not looked upon as a bowler – even for a change. He afterwards, however, greatly improved; and what with his thorough knowledge of the game, his crafty manner (for he was one of the most fox-headed fellows I ever saw), and his quickness in seizing every advantage, he was of considerable service to his party, but he never was a first-rate bowler. He was a right, and Harry a left-handed batter, and both were valuable men. They came from Thursley, near Hindhead; they and their father were farmers, and their land lay near to the Devil's Punch-bowl.

The next in succession will be JOHN WELLS, the BELDHAMS, HARRIS, and FREEMANTLE.

Shortly after the Walkers had joined us, JOHN WELLS became a member of the Hambledon Club. John lived at Farnham, in Surrey, and was, if I recollect, a baker by trade. He was a short, thick, well-set man; in make like a cob-horse, proportionately strong, active, and laborious. As a bowler, he had a very good delivery; he was also a good general field, and a steady batter – in short, an excellent 'servant of all work'; and, like those misused Gibeonites ('hewers of wood and drawers of water'), he was never spared when a wear-and-tear post was to be occupied. In cricket, as in the graver pursuits of life, the willing workman is ever spurred; he may perform labours of supererogation, and his assiduity meets at best with 'mouth honour': let him, however, but relax his muscles – let him but shorten his career to the speed of his fellows, and he instantly sinks below them in the estimation of his employers. Whether in this case, the feeling arise from envy or not, it is hard to decide; assuredly, however, in very many instances, the mill-horse grinder in the track of duty is acknowledged with greeting, while extra merit 'goes out sighing.' John Wells possessed all the requisites for making a thoroughly useful cricketer; and in his general deportment, he was endowed with those qualities which render man useful to society as well as happy in himself. He was a creature of a transparent and unflawed integrity – plain, simple and candid; uncompromising, yet courteous: civil and deferential, yet no cringer. He always went by the title of 'Honest John Wells,' and as long as I knew him, he never forfeited the character he had gained. Little more need be added respecting his merits as a player, for he must be fresh in the memory of all who have been accustomed to see the best playing; suffice to say, that in addition to his level merits as a general cricketer, he was esteemed to possess an excellent judgement of the game, and in questions that were frequently mooted, his opinion would be appealed to.

The BELDHAMS, GEORGE and WILLIAM, come next in succession, brothers, and both farmers. They also with Wells came from Farnham. George was what would be called a fine player; a good batter, and generally competent to fill the different posts in the game; but as he attended the club only a few times only during my stay in it, I am unable to discriminate or speak pointedly to his merits. Upon turning, however, to his brother, William, we come to the finest batter of his own, or perhaps of any age. William Beldham was a close-set, active man, standing about five feet eight inches and a half. He had light-coloured hair, a fair complexion, and handsome as well as intelligent features. We used to call him 'Silver Billy.' No one within my recollection could stop a ball better, or make more brilliant hits all over the ground. Wherever the ball was bowled, there she was hit away, and in the most severe, venomous style. Besides this, he was so remarkably safe a player; he was safer than the Bank, for no mortal ever thought of doubting Beldham's stability. He received his instructions from a ginger-bread baker at Farnham, of the name of Harry Hall. I once played against Hall, and found him a very fair hand, yet nothing remarkable; he knew the principles of the game, yet, like many of inferior merit in performance, he made nevertheless an excellent tutor. He was a slow bowler, and a pretty good one. He had a peculiar habit of bringing his hand from behind his back immediately previous to his delivering the ball, a trick no doubt perplexing enough to an inexperienced batter. In his peripatetic lectures to the young students, Hall perpetually enforced the principle of keeping the *left* elbow well up (this charge was of course delivered to the *right*-handed hitters), and excellent instruction it was; for if you do keep that elbow well up, and your bat also upright (in stopping a *length-ball*), you will not fail to keep the balls *down*; and, *vice versa,* lower your elbow, and your balls will infallibly mount when you strike them.

BELDHAM was quite a young man when he joined the Hambledon Club; and even in that stage of his playing, I hardly ever saw a man with a finer command of his bat; but, with the instruction and advice of the old heads superadded, he rapidly attained to the extraordinary accomplishment of being the finest player that has appeared within the latitude of more than half a century. There can be no exception against his batting, or the severity of his hitting. He would get in at the balls, and hit them away in a gallant style; yet, in this single feat, I think I have known him excelled; but when he could cut them at the point of his bat, he was in his glory; and upon my life their speed

was as the speed of thought. One of the most beautiful sights
than can be imagined, and which would have delighted an
artist, was to see him make himself up to hit a ball. It was
the beau-ideal of grace, animation and concentrated energy.
In this peculiar exhibition of elegance with vigour, the
nearest approach to him, I think, was Lord Frederick
Beauclerck. Upon one occasion at Mary-le-bone, I remember these two admirable batters being in together, and
though Beldham was then verging towards his climacteric,
yet both were excited to a competition, and the display
of talent that was exhibited between them that day was the
most interesting sight of its kind I ever witnessed. I should
not forget, among his other excellences, to mention that
Beldham was one of the best judges of a short run I ever
knew, add to which, that he possessed a generally good
knowledge of the game.

Hitherto I have spoken only of his batting. In this department alone, he had talent enough to make a dozen
ordinary cricketers, but as a general fieldsman there were
few better; he could take any post in the field, and do
himself credit in it: latterly he usually chose the place of
slip. But Beldham was a good change-bowler too; he
delivered his balls high, and they got up well. His pace
was a moderate one, yet bordering upon the quick. His
principal fault in this department was, that he would often
give a toss; taking him, however, as a change-bowler, he
was one of the best. He would very quickly discover what a
hitter could do, and what he could not do, and arrange
his bowling accordingly. Finally, although his balls were
commonly to the length, he was much better calculated for
a change than to be continued a considerable length of
time.

One of the finest treats in cricketing that I remember,
was to see this admirable man in, with the beautiful bowling of Harris.

Having finished with the best batter of his own, or,
perhaps, of any age – Beldham, we proceed to the very best
bowler; a bowler who, between any one and himself,
comparison must fail. DAVID HARRIS was I believe, born,
at all events he lived, at Odiham in Hampshire; he was

by trade a potter. He was a muscular, bony man, standing
about five feet nine and a half inches. His features were
not regularly handsome, but a remarkably kind and gentle
expression amply compensated the deffect of mere linear
beauty. The fair qualities of his heart shone through his
honest face, and I can call to mind no worthier, or, in the
active sense of the word, not a more '*good* man' than David
Harris. He was one of the rare species that link man to
man in bonds of fellowship by good works; that inspire
confidence, and prevent the structure of society from be-
coming disjointed, and, 'as it were, a bowing wall, or a
tottering fence.' He was a man of so strict a principal, and
such high honour, that I believe his moral character was
never impeached. I never heard even a suspicion breathed
against his integrity, and I knew him long and intimately. I
do not mean that he was a *canter*. – Oh, no – no one thought
of standing on guard, and buttoning up his pockets in
Harris's company. I never busied myself about his mode
of faith, or the peculiarity of his creed; that was his own
affair, not mine, or any other being's on earth; all I know
is, that he was an '*honest man,*' and the poet has assigned
the rank of such a one in creation.

It would be difficult, perhaps impossible, to convey in
writing an accurate idea of the grand effect of Harris's
bowling; they only who have played against him can fully
appreciate it. His attitude when preparing for his run
previously to delivering the ball, would have made a beautiful study for the sculptor. Phidias would certainly have
taken him for a model. First of all, he stood erect like a
soldier at drill; then, with a graceful curve of the arm,
he raised the ball to his forehead, and drawing back his
right foot, started off with his left. The calm look and
general air of the man were uncommonly striking, and
from this series of preparations he never deviated. I am sure
that from this simple account of his manner, all my country-
men who were acquainted with his play will recall him to
their minds. His mode of delivering the ball was very
singular. He would bring it from under the arm by a twist,
and nearly as high as his arm-pit, and with this action *push*
it, as it were, from him. How it was that the balls acquired

the velocity they did by this mode of delivery I never could comprehend.

When first he joined the Hambledon Club, he was quite a raw countryman at cricket, and had very little to recommend him but his noble delivery. He was also very apt to give tosses. I have seen old Nyren scratch his head, and say – 'Harris would make the best bowler in England if he did not toss.' By continual practice, however, and following the advice of the old Hambledon players, he became as steady as could be wished; and in the prime of his playing very rarely indeed gave a toss, although his balls were pitched the full length. In bowling, he never stooped in the least in his delivery, but kept himself upright all the time. His balls were very little beholden to the ground when pitched; it was but a touch, and up again; and woe be to the man who did not get in to block them, for they had such a peculiar curl, that they would grind his fingers against the bat; many a time have I seen the blood drawn in this way from a batter who was not up to the trick; old Tom Walker was the only exception – I have before classed him among the bloodless animals.

Harris's bowling was the finest of all tests for a hitter, and hence the great beauty, as I observed before, of seeing Beldham in, with this man against him; for unless a batter were of the very first class, and accustomed to the best style of stopping, he could do little or nothing with Harris. If the thing had been possible, I should have liked to have seen such a player as Budd (fine hitter as he was) standing against him. My own opinion is, that he could not have stopped his balls, and this will be a criterion, by which those who have seen some of that gentleman's brilliant hits, may judge of the extraordinary merit of this man's bowling. He was considerably faster than Lambert, and so superior in style and finish, that I can draw no comparison between them. Lord Frederick Beauclerck has been heard to say that Harris's bowling was one of the grandest things of the kind he had ever seen; but his Lordship could not have known him in his prime; he never saw him play till after he had had many fits of the gout, and had become slow and feeble.

To Harris's fine bowling I attribute the great improvement that was made in hitting, and above all in stopping; for its was utterly impossible to remain at the crease, when the ball was tossed to a fine length; you were obliged to get in, or it would be about your hands, or the handle of your bat; and every player knows where its next place would be.

Some years after Harris had played with the Hambledon Club, he became so well acquainted with the science of the game of cricket, that he could take a very great advantage in pitching the wickets. And not only would he pitch a good wicket for himself, but he would also consider those who had to bowl with him. The writer of this had often walked with him up to Windmill-down at six o'clock in the morning of the day that a match was to be played, and has with pleasure noticed the pains he has taken in choosing the ground for his fellow-bowler as well as himself. The most eminent men in every walk of life have at all times been the most painstaking; – slabberdash work and indifference may accompany genius, and it does so too frequently; such geniuses, however, throw away more than half their chance. There are more brilliant talents in this world than people give the world credit for; and that their lustre does not exhibit to the best advantage, commonly depends upon the owners of them. Ill luck, and the preference that frequently attends industrious mediocrity, are the only anodynes that wounded self-love or indolence can administer to misapplied or unused ability. In his walk, Harris was a man of genius, and he let slip no opportunity to maintain his pre-eminence. Although unwilling to detract from the fame of old Lumpy, I must here observe upon the difference in these two men with regard to pitching their wickets. Lumpy would uniformly select a point where the ball was likely to shoot, that is, over the brow of a little hill; and when by this forethought and contrivance, the old man would prove successful in bowling his men out, he would turn round to his party with a little grin of triumph; nothing gratified him like this reward of his knowingness. Lumpy, however, thought only of himself in choosing his ground; his fellow-bowler might take his chance; this was neither wise nor liberal. Harris, on the contrary, as I have already observed, considered his partner; and, in so doing, the main chance of the game. Unlike Lumpy, too, he would choose a rising ground to pitch the ball against, and he who is well acquainted with the game of cricket will at once perceive the advantage that must arise from a wicket pitched in this way to such a tremendous bowler as Harris was. If I were urged to draw a comparison between these two great players, the greatest certainly in their department I ever saw, I could do it in no other way than the following: – Lumpy's ball was always pitched to the length, but delivered lower than Harris's, and never got up so high; he was also slower than Harris, and lost his advantage by the way in which he persisted in pitching his wicket; yet I think he would bowl more wickets down than the other, for the latter never pitched his wicket with this end in view; almost all his balls, therefore, rose over the wicket; consequently, more players would be caught out from Harris than Lumpy, and not half the number of runs got from his bowling. I passed a very pleasant time with Harris when he came to my father's house at Hambledon, by invitation, after an illness, and for the benefit of the change of air. Being always his companion in his walks about the neighbourhood, I had full opportunity of observing the sweetness of his disposition; this, with his manly contempt of every action that bore the character of meanness, gained him the admiration of every cricketer in Hambledon.

In concluding my recollection of Harris, I had well-nigh omitted to say something of his skill in the other departments of the game. The fact is, the extraordinary merit of his bowling would have thrown any other fair accomplishment he might possess into the shade; but, indeed, as a batter, I considered him rather an indifferent hand; I never recollect his getting more than ten runs, and those very rarely. Neither was his fielding remarkable. But he was game to the backbone, and never suffered a ball to pass him without putting his body in the way of it. If I recollect, he generally played slip.

The FREEMANTLES. There were two of them, and, I

believe, brothers. JOHN and ANDREW were their names. One was an acknowledged player long before the other began. I am now, however, speaking of Freemantle the bowler. He, with Andrew, came from some town between Winchester and Alresford. John was a stoutly-made man; his standard about five feet ten inches. He delivered his ball high and well, and tolerably fast, yet he could not be ranked among the *fast* bowlers. The best compliment I can pay him is, that he was reckoned very successful, and, moreover, that his being a member of the Hambledon Club was sufficient guarantee for his general ability, as those sound and experienced judges would never admit as a member any man who did not possess some qualifications above the common level.

As a batter, John Freemantle would have been reckoned a good hand in any club. He would now and then get many runs; yet withal, he could by no means be pronounced a *fine* batter. As a man, he bore a high character for straightforward, manly integrity; in short, he was a hearty John Bull, and flinched no more from his duty than he did from a ball in the field, and this he never did, however hard it might hit him.

Andrew was a shortish, well-set man, and a left-handed player. He was an uncommonly safe, as well as good hitter; and few wickets that I could name were more secure than Andrew's. He would often get long hands, and against the best bowling too; and when he had once warmed into his hitting, it was a deuced hard matter to get him out – an accident would frequently do the business. In his general style of batting he very much reminded me of Aylward, who has been spoken of some pages back. He usually played the long field, and was remarkably steady and safe in this department. But Andrew Freemantle could be depended upon, whatever he might undertake, whether in cricket or in his worldly dealings.

Upon one occasion when I had come up to London, I heard of a match being played in Lord's Ground, and of course made one of the spectator's of my beloved amusement. Andrew Freemantle was in, and one of the new-fashioned bowlers, commonly called throwers, was bowling

to him. His name was WILLES, and I believe he came out of
Sussex. He was the first I had seen of the new school,
after the Walkers had attempted to introduce the system
in the Hambledon Club. Willes frequently pitched his balls
to the off-side of the wicket to Freemantle's left-handed
hitting, who got in before the wicket, and hit the thrower's
bowling behind him. Now, had he missed the ball, and it
had hit his leg, although before the wicket, he would not
have been out, because it had been pitched at the outside
of the off-stump. I mention this trifling circumstance to
show the knowledge the latter had of the game.

Andrew Freemantle's fielding was very fair; his post was
generally the long field. He, however, must be so well
known to many of the Mary-le-bone men now living, that
I need enumerate no more of the peculiar characteristics of
his playing.

Next comes that deservedly esteemed character, JOHN
SMALL, son and worthy successor to the celebrated batter
of the same name. He, as well as his father, was a native
of Petersfield. Young Small was a very handsomely-made
man. For perfect symmetry of form, and well-knit, compact
limbs and frame, his father was one of the finest models
of a man I had ever beheld; and the son was little inferior
to him in any respect. Jack Small! my old club fellow!
when the fresh and lusty Maytide of life sent the blood
gamboling through our veins like a Spring runlet, we have
had many a good bout together:

'But now my head is bald, John,
And locks as white as snow,' –

and yours have, doubtless, bleached under the cold hand
of mayhap three-score winters and more; but the churl has
not yet touched the citadel. *My* heart is as sound as ever,
and beats regular and true time to the tune of old and
grateful thoughts for long friendships. You, I am sure, can
echo this sentiment. You are a musician as well as a friend,
and know the value of steadiness in both characters. I think
we could give some of the young whipsters a little trouble
even now. Like the old Knight of the Boar's Head, we
might need the *legs* of these Harry Monmouths; but it is

my opinion we could bother them yet, at a good stand to our post. They would find some trouble to bowl down our stumps. They say, Jack, you were born with a bat in your hand. I can believe the tale, for I am sure you in-herited the craft from both father and mother. She, I think, took as much delight and interest in the game as he. Many's the time I have seen that worthy woman (every way deserv-ing of so kind and excellent a husband) come galloping up the ground at a grand match, where he was to play (for, you know, she always accompanied him to those high solemnities), and no player even could show more interest in the progress of the game than she, and certainly no one, as was natural, felt so much pride in her husband's fine playing.

I do not remember, John, that you were much of a bowler, but I remember that you were everything else, and that your judgement of the game was equal to that of any man. Your style of hitting, to my mind, was of the very first quality; and I can name no one who possessed a more accurate judgement of a short run. By the bye – is that account true which I have heard, that upon one occasion, at Mary-le-bone, you and Hammond went in first, when there were only forty runs to get to win the match; and that you made an agreement together to run whenever the ball passed the wicket-keeper: that you did this, and between you got the whole forty runs before you were out? I have been told this anecdote of you both, and, if true, it clearly shows, according to my opinion, that the judgement of the people who played against you must have been strangely at fault, or they might have prevented it; for had but the long-stop been well acquainted with the game, he would have put you out.

I always admired your fielding, Jack: I am not sure that your middle wicket (the post that your father occupied) was not as good as his – though, I dare say, you would not allow this. Certain am I that a better never was put at the post. And now, farewell, my old club-fellow.

Reader! in a few words (now he has left the room), I assure you that in every way he was as complete a chap as I ever knew – a genuine chip of the old block – an admirable player, and a highly honourable man. The legs at Mary-le-bone never produced the least change in him; but, on the contrary, he was thoroughly disgusted at some of the manoeuvres that took place there from time to time.

About the time that John Small had risen into the celebrity I have just been describing, his father and Nyren retired from the field. I cannot do better, in concluding these brief recollections, than enumerate the most eminent players in the Hambledon Club when it was in its glory.

DAVID HARRIS	TOM WALKER
JOHN WELLS	—— ROBINSON
—— PURCHASE	NOAH MANN
WILLIAM BELDHAM	—— SCOTT
JOHN SMALL, JUN.	—— TAYLOR
HARRY WALKER	

No eleven in England could have had any chance with these men; and I think they might have beaten any two-and-twenty.

A FEW MEMORANDA RESPECTING THE

PROGRESS OF CRICKET

M R Ward obligingly furnished me with a small MS., written some years since by an old cricketer, containing a few hasty recollections and rough hints to players, thrown together without regard to method or order. From the mass, I have been able to select a few portions, thinking that they might possess some interest with those of my readers who take a pride in the game.

From the authority before me, it appears that about 150 years since, it was the custom, as at present, to pitch the wickets at the same distance asunder, viz., twenty-two yards. That the stumps (only one foot high, and two feet* wide) were surmounted with a bail. At that period, however

* There must be a mistake in this account of the *width* of the wicket—J. N.

another peculiarity in the game was in practice, and which
it is worthwhile to record. Between the stumps a hole was
cut in the ground, large enough to contain the ball and the
butt-end of the bat. In running a notch, the striker was
required to put his bat into this hole, instead of the
modern practice of touching over the popping-crease. The
wicket-keeper, in putting out the striker when running, was
obliged, when the ball was thrown in, to place it in this hole
before the adversary could reach it with his bat. Many
severe injuries of the hands were the consequence of this
regulation; the present mode of touching the popping-
crease was therefore substituted for it. At the same period
the wickets were increased to twenty-two inches in height,
and six inches in breadth, and instead of the old custom of
placing the ball in the hole, the wicket-keeper was required
to put the wicket down, having the ball in his hand.

The following account of a match played in the year
1744 has been selected by the writer above mentioned, in
order to show the state of play at that time. It arose from a
challenge given by Lord John Sackville on the part of the
County of Kent to play all England; and it proved to be a
well-contested match, as will appear from the manner in
which the players kept the field. The hitting, however,
could neither have been of a high character, nor indeed
safe, as may be gathered from the figure of the bat at that
time; which was similar to an old-fashioned dinner-knife
– curved at the back, and sweeping in the form of a volute
at the front and end. With such a bat, the system must have
been all for hitting; it would be barely possible to block:
and when the practice of bowling length-balls was introduced and which gave the bowler so great an advantage
in the game, it became absolutely necessary to change the
form of the bat, in order that the striker might be able to
keep pace with the improvement. It was therefore made
straight in the pod; in consequence of which, a total revo-
lution, it may be said a reformation too, ensued in the style
of play.

The following is the record of the match alluded to: –

KENT AGAINST ALL ENGLAND

PLAYED IN THE ARTILLERY GROUND, LONDON

ENGLAND

	1st Innings Runs			2nd Innings Runs		
Harris	0	B by	Hadswell	4	B by	Mills
Dingate	3	B	do	11	B	Hadswell
Newland	0	B	Mills	3	B	do
Cuddy	0	B	Hadswell	2	C	Danes
Green	0	B	Mills	5	B	Mills
Waymark	7	B	do	9	B	Hadswell
Bryan	12	S	Kips	7	C	Kips
Newland	18	—	not out	15	C	Lord J. Sackville
Harris	0	B	Hadswell	1	B	Hadswell
Smith	0	C	Bartrum	8	B	Mills
Newland	0	B	Mills	5	—	not out
	Byes 0			Byes 0		
	40			70		

KENT

	1st Innings Runs			2nd Innings Runs		
Lord J. Sackville	5	C by	Waymark	3	B by	Harris
Long Robin	7	B	Newland	9	B	Newland
Mills	0	B	Harris	6	C	do
Hadswell	0	B	do	5	—	not out
Cutbush	3	C	Green	7	—	not out
Bartrum	2	B	Newland	0	B	Newland
Danes	6	B	do	0	C	Smith
Sawyer	0	C	Waymark	5	B	Newland
Kips	12	B	Harris	10	B	Harris
Mills	7	—	not out	2	B	Newland
Romney	11	B	Harris	8	C	Harris
	Byes 0			Byes 3		
	53			58		

Some years after this, the fashion of the bat having been changed to a straight form, the system of stopping, or blocking, was adopted; when JOHN SMALL, Sen., of Petersfield, in Hampshire, became signalised as the most eminent

batsman of his day, being a very safe player, and a remarkably fine hitter: and EDWARD STEVENS, or, as he was
commonly called, LUMPY, was esteemed the best bowler.

About the years 1769 and 1770, the Hambledon Club,
having had a run of ill success was on the eve of being
dissolved. It had been hitherto supported by the most
respectable gentlemen in that part of the county. They
determined, however, once more to try their fortune, and on
the 23rd of September 1771, having played the County of
Surrey, at Laleham Burway, they beat them by one run.
Out of fifty-one matches played by the same club against
England, &c., during the ensuing ten years, they gained
twenty-nine of the number.

Several years since (I do not recollect the precise date)
a player, named White, of Ryegate, brought a bat to a
match, which being the width of the stumps, effectually
defended his wicket from the bowler: and, in consequence,
a law was passed limiting the future width of the bat to
$4\frac{1}{4}$* inches. Another law also decreed that the ball should
not weigh less than $5\frac{1}{2}$ oz., or more than $5\frac{3}{4}$ oz.

On the 22nd of May 1775, a match was played in the
Artillery Ground, between five of the Hambledon Club,
and five of all England; when Small went in the last man
for fourteen runs, and fetched them. Lumpy was bowler
upon the occasion; and it having been remarked that his
balls had three several times passed between Small's stumps,
it was considered to be a hard thing upon the bowler that
his straightest balls should be thus sacrificed; the number
of the stumps was in consequence increased from two to
three. Many amateurs were of opinion at the time, that the
alteration would tend to shorten the game: and subsequently, the Hampshire gentlemen did me the honour of
taking my opinion upon this point. I agreed with them that
it was but doing justice to the bowler; but I differed
upon the question that it would shorten the game; because

---

* I have a perfect recollection of this occurrence; also, that
subsequently, an iron frame, of the statute width, was constructed
for, and kept by the Hambledon Club; through which any bat
of suspected dimensions was passed, and allowed or rejected
accordingly – J. N.

the striker, knowing the danger of missing one straight ball with three instead of two stumps behind him, would materially redouble his care; while every loose, hard hitter would learn to stop, and play as safe a game as possible. The following record of a match, played shortly afterwards between the Hambledon Club and All England, at Seven-oaks, will prove whether my opinion were well or ill founded.

It was upon this occasion that Aylward fetched the extra-ordinary number of 167 runs from his own bat; – one of the greatest feats upon record in the annals of cricket; for, it must be borne in mind, that his success did not arise from any loose playing or incompetence on the part of his opponents – there would then have been no merit in the triumph; but he had to stand against the finest bowling of the day – that of Lumpy.

The reader will not fail likewise to remark the difference of amount in the score between the first and second innings on the England side; the men were either disheartened at the towering pre-eminence of the adverse party; or, which is more probable, the latter, like good generals, would not throw away a single chance; but although the odds were so greatly in their favour, they, instead of relaxing, or show-ing any indifference, fielded with still greater care than in the first innings; and, in consequence, their opponents did not score half their previous number of runs. This is the genuine spirit of emulation.

HAMBLEDON CLUB AGAINST ALL ENGLAND
PLAYED 18TH JUNE 1777

ENGLAND

	1st Innings Runs			2nd Innings Runs		
Duke of Dorset	0	B by Brett		5	C by Ld. Tankerville	
Lumpy	1	B	do	2	—	not out
Wood	1	B	do	1	B	Nyren
White	8	C	Veck	10	—	not out
Miller	27	C	Small	23	B	Brett
Minchin*	60	—	not out	12	B	Taylor
Bowra	2	B	Brett	4	B	do
Bullen	13	C	Ld. Tankerville	2	B	Nyren
Booker	8	C	Brett	2	B	Brett
Yalden	6	C	Small	8	C	Nyren
Pattenden	38	B	Brett	0	C	Brett
Byes	2			0		
	166			69		

* Minshull

HAMBLEDON

	1st innings Runs		
Lord Tankerville	3	B by Wood	
Leer	7		do
Veck	16	B	Lumpy
Small	33	C	White
Francis	26	C	Wood
Nyren	37	B	Lumpy
Sueter	46	B	Wood
Taylor	32	C	Bullen
Aburrow	22	C	Minchin
Aylward	167	B	Bullen
Brett	9	—	not out
Byes	5		
	403		

Won by Hambledon by 168 runs in *one* innings.

In the year 1778, HARRIS, the best bowler ever known, began playing in the first matches; and from the vast superiority of his style, the hitting increased both in safety and severity, particularly in Hampshire and Surrey, where the players had an opportunity of practising against the bowling of this remarkable man. He had a very high delivery of the balls, and was as steady to a length. This obliged the striker to play forward, otherwise, from the rapidity of the balls rising from the ground, he was sure to be caught out at the point of the bat. I consider cricket to have been at its zenith at the time that Harris was in prime play.

Afer his death a childish mode of bowling was adopted; very slow and high, and scarcely passing the wicket. By some, the ball was delivered with a straight arm, nearly approaching to a gentle throw. That practice, however (of throwing), was set aside by a resolution of the Mary-le-bone Club.*

[Here follow some general instructions to the bowler and striker; they are, however, brief, and at the same time bear so closely upon those already given in previous pages of this little work, that the inserting of them would amount almost to a verbal repetition.

The following hints to the directors and managers of a match will amuse some readers, and not be wholly unworthy the attention of those who are ambitious of playing a keen and manoeuvring, rather than a plain and straightforward game.]

MANAGEMENT OF A MATCH

In making a match, you should be careful to stand on higher terms than you have an absolute occasion for; that you may the more easily obtain such as are necessary; keeping in mind the old adage – 'A match well made is half won.'

* Tom Walker was the first to introduce the system of throwing; and it was to provide against such an innovation that the law was passed, and which law is still in force, although it is daily infringed, and will, in all probability, become a dead letter–J. N.

In pitching the wickets* when it falls to your lot to have the pitching of them, you must be careful to suit your bowling. If you have one slow, and one fast bowler, pitch your wickets right up and down the wind. A slow bowler can never bowl well with the wind in his face. If your bowling is all fast, and your opponents have a slow bowler, pitch your wickets with a cross wind, that you may in some degree destroy the effect of the slow bowling. If either of your bowlers twists his balls, favour such twist as much as possible by taking care to choose the ground at that spot where the ball should pitch its proper length, a little sloping inwards.

If you go in first, let two of your most safe and steady players be put in, that you may stand a chance of *'milling'* the bowling in the early part of the game. And whenever a man is put out, and if the bowling have become loose, put in a resolute hard hitter. Observe also, if two players are well in, and warm with getting runs fast, and one should be put out, that you supply his place immediately, lest the other become cold and stiff.

When your party takes the field, let your bowlers take full time between their balls, keeping a close field till your opponents begin to hit freely, when you must extend your men as occasion may require.

If the opposite party hold in, and are getting runs too fast, change your worst bowler, being careful at the same time to bring forward one as opposite to him as possible, both in speed and delivery. If you bring forward a fast bowler as a change, contrive, if fortune so favour you, that he shall bowl his first ball *when a cloud is passing over*; because as this trifling circumstance frequently affects the sight of a striker, you may thereby stand a good chance of getting him out.

When it is difficult to part two batsmen and either of them has a favourite hit, I have often succeeded in getting him out by opening the field where his hit is placed, at the same time hinting to the bowler to give him a different style of ball. This, with the opening of the field, has

* Now the province of the umpires: see copy of the Laws.

tempted him to plant his favourite hit, and in his anxiety to do so has not unfrequently committed an error fatal to him.

Every manoeuvre must be tried in a desperate state of the game; but, above all things, be slow and steady, being also especially careful that your field do not become confused. Endeavour by every means in your power — such as, by changing the bowling, by little alterations in the field, or by any excuse you can invent, to delay the time, that the strikers may become cold and inactive. And when you get a turn in your favour, you may push on the game a little faster; but even then be not too flushed with success, but let your play be still cool, cautious, and steady.

If your party go in the last innings for a certain number of runs always keep back two or three of your safest batsmen for the last wickets. Timid or hazardous hitters seldom do so well when the game is desperate, as those who, from safe play, are more confident.

LIST OF THE MEMBERS

OF THE

MARY-LE-BONE CLUB

Acheson, Viscount
Adamson, Mr
Aislabie, Mr B.
Anderson, Mr
Anderson, Mr D.
Ashley, Hon. H.
Antrobus, Mr J.
Baker, Mr
Barclay, Mr R.
Barham, Mr
Barham, Mr W.
Barnard, Mr
Barnett, Mr James
Barnett, Mr Charles
Barnett, Mr G. H.
Bathurst, Sir F.
Bayley, Mr J.
Beauclerck, Lord F.
Beauclerck, Mr
Bearblock, Mr W.
Belfast, Earl of
Bennett, Mr
Berens, Mr R.
Biddulph, Mr R. M.
Bligh, Hon. Gen.
Brooke, Mr F. C.
Brooks, Mr
Budd, Mr
Balfour, Captain
Blake, Mr J. G.
Caldwell, Mr
Caldwell, Mr B.
Calmady, Mr
Campbell, Mr
Castlereagh, Lord
Cheslyn, Mr
Chesterfield, Earl of
Chichester, Earl of

Clitheroe, Mr J. C.
Codrington, Captain
Colcomb, Major
Cope, Sir John, Bart.
Cotton, Sir St Vincent
Cox, Mr
Clonbrock, Lord
Cox, Mr C.
Curtis, Sir William
Curzon, Hon. F.
Clayton, Captain
Darnley, Earl of
Davidson, Mr H.
Davidson, Mr D.
Davidson, Mr W.
Davidson, Captain
Deedes, Mr W.
Deedes, Mr James
Delme, Mr C.
Denne, Mr T.
Dunlo, Lord
Dyke, Mr P. H.
Dillon, Hon. Mr
Ellis, Mr W.
Ellis, Mr C.
Everett, Mr
Exeter, Marquis of
Fairfield, Mr G.
Fairlie, Mr
Fairlie, Mr W.
Fitzroy, Mr H.
Forbes, Mr
Franklyn, Mr
Fryer, Mr
Fuller, Mr
Finch, Hon. D.
Flayer, Mr
Gardiner, Colonel

Gaselee, Mr
Gibbon, Sir John, Bart.
Glenorchy, Lord
Gordon, Hon. Fred.
Gordon, Hon. Francis
Goring, Mr F.
Greenwood, Captain (2nd Life
    Guards)
Greenwood, Captain (Grenadier
    Guards)
Greville, Captain
Greville, Hon. R. F.
Grey, Lord
Grimstead, Mr
Grimston, Lord
Grimston, Hon. E. H.
Gunning, Sir R. H., Bart.
Hale, Mr C.
Harman, Mr E. D.
Harrington, Mr
Heathcote, Mr J. M.
Hemming, Mr
Hill, Mr C.
Hill, Mr P.
Hillsborough, Earl of
Hoare, Mr
Howard, Mr
Harbord, Hon. E. V.
*Jenner, Mr H.
Jones, Mr D. H.
Johnson, Mr
Keen, Mr
Kingscote, Mr H.
Knatchbull, Mr
Knight, Mr E.
Knight, Mr G. T.
Kynaston, Mr
Labalmondiere, Mr
Ladbrook, Mr F.
Lascelles, Hon. Col.
Lascelles, Hon. E.
Leathes, Mr
Lloyd, Mr H.
Lloyd, Mr C.
Loftus, Captain
Long, Colonel
Lowther, Hon. Col.
Mackinnon, Mr H.

M'Taggert, Mr T.
Mann, Colonel
Mallet, Sir Alexander
Martyn, Mr
Mellish, Mr T.
Meyrick, Mr F.
Mills, Mr E.
Mills, Mr C.
Montague, Hon. S. D.
Moreton, Hon. H.
Morgan, Mr W. H.
Musgrave, Captain
Michel, Captain
Nicole, Mr
Northy, Captain
Oglander, Mr
Onslow, Mr G.
Ossory, Lord
Phillimore, Captain
Pack, Mr
Parry, Mr F.
Paul, Sir D., Bart.
Paul, Mr
Payne, Mr G.
Pickering, Mr
Philipps, Mr
Plunket, Mr
Plymouth, Earl of
Pocklington, Mr
Ponsonby, Hon. G.
Powell, Mr J. H., jun.
Purling, Mr
Payne, Mr A.
Pigott, Mr W. P.
Quarme, Mr
Reed, Mr
Ricardo, Mr
Robarts, Mr
Romilly, Mr E.
Romilly, Mr C.
Romilly, Mr F.
Rothschild, Mr
Russell, Lord C.
St. Albans, Duke of
Scott, Mr J. W.
Scott, Hon. W.
Sewell, Colonel
Shelley, Mr

* Mr Herbert Jenner, now Mr Jenner-Fust, is the only person
mentioned in this list who still survives. He was born in Sackville Street, London, February 23, 1806.—Ed.

Sivewright, Mr E.
Sivewright, Mr C. K.
Stanley, Hon. Capt. Thomas
Stone, Mr R.
Stonor, Mr
Strahan, Mr
Strathavon, Lord
Stubbs, Mr
Sullivan, Mr
Smith, Mr
Talbot, Hon. Mr
Tanner, Mr
Thynne, Lord W.
Townsend, Mr
Trevanion, Mr
Turner, Mr
Uxbridge, Earl of
Vigne, Mr

Vigne, Mr G. T.
Villiers, Hon. A.
Vivian, Mr
Vincent, Sir F.
Walker, Mr E.
Walpole, Mr R.
Walton, Mr
Ward, Mr W.
Waterpark, Lord
Webster, Colonel
Wells, Mr J.
Willan, Mr
Wodehouse, Mr
Wood, Mr
Wright, Mr J. D.
Walker, Mr H.
Willoughby, Sir H.